# Praise for
# *Mission Metamorphosis*

"A perfect title at the perfect time for the perfect account of selfless-
ness, rescue, and humanity. We all should take a page from *Mission
Metamorphosis* and effect change, positively, tangibly, and personally."

**–MAJOR GENERAL (RET.) JAMES. A. "SPIDER" MARKS**

"*Mission Metamorphosis* tells the story of American Humane's radical
rescue from the peril of insolvency, and the hard work that went into
re-establishing the historic organization as a leader in the humane
space. Today, the organization continues to deliver on its mission and
improve the lives of animals around the world. 'First to serve' could be
renamed 'Always and forever serve!'"

**–MARTY BECKER, DVM**

"*Mission Metamorphosis* is a no-nonsense, practical guide on managing
a nonprofit so that it achieves its mission, gets things done, and avoids
wasting money on excessive administrative costs."

**–TEMPLE GRANDIN, PhD**

"At a time when species on every continent are in danger, American Humane is delivering on its mission to improve the lives of animals. *Mission Metamorphosis* shows how the 143-year-old nonprofit operates with maximum efficiency to help animals in need. A must-read for all business leaders concerned about animal welfare."

—WOLFGANG KIESSLING, *founder and president of Loro Parque*

"For success, it is essential that all operations within an organization be laser-focused on mission. *Mission Metamorphosis* is a masterclass on how to fine-tune a nonprofit organization and for-profit company to maximize efficiency and deliver real change to constituencies."

—JEAN SHAFIROFF, *philanthropist and author of*
*Successful Philanthropy: How to Make a Life By What You Give*

"*Mission Metamorphosis* brings to life the incredible work of American Humane and its outstanding leader—which I have been privileged to participate in and observe firsthand."

—ALEX DONNER, *philanthropist and entertainer*

"Robin's turnaround of American Humane has been a tour de force, and saved the lives literally of millions of animals around the world. *Mission Metamorphosis* is a strategic and sweeping account of how she did it, and serves as a captivating example for other nonprofit leaders of what authentic and visionary leadership brings to an organization. Like Robin herself, *Mission Metamorphosis* is down-to-earth, dynamic, inspiring, and looks you straight in the eye. Share this with your leadership team and watch the transformation unfold!"

—MARK CUSHING, *founding partner and*
*CEO of Animal Policy Group*

"*Mission Metamorphosis* is a great read for many reasons. Robin Ganzert is a fascinating storyteller as she recounts American Humane's rich history of disaster missions and animal rescue efforts. She's also a brilliant CEO who knows that a brand's mission can only be a success if it's built upon a sound foundation of essential business strategies. This book is a how-to guide for nonprofit leaders interested in transformational leadership. It will help empower them to effect positive change in the world, whether leading a nationwide organization or looking to make an impact in their local community. Thank you, Robin, for giving us tools for building a more compassionate world!"

–BARBARA NIVEN, *actress and animal and human rights advocate*

"For 143 years, American Humane has been first to serve animals, whenever and wherever they are in need. *Mission Metamorphosis* tells how the organization continued to deliver on its mission in the wake of the 2008 recession. A powerful story of rebirth!"

—DANIELLE FISHEL, *actress*

★ Leadership for a Humane World ★

# MISSION
## METAMORPHOSIS

Robin R. Ganzert, PhD

FAST
COMPANY
*Press*

Fast Company Press
New York, New York
www.fastcompanypress.com

Distributed by Greenleaf Book Group

For ordering information or special discounts for bulk purchases, please contact Greenleaf Book Group at PO Box 91869, Austin, TX 78709, 512.891.6100.

Design and composition by Greenleaf Book Group
Cover design by Greenleaf Book Group
Cover Images: ©iStockphoto/Counterfeit_ua and ©iStockphoto/filo

Publisher's Cataloging-in-Publication data is available.

Print ISBN: 978-1-7324391-8-4

eBook ISBN: 978-1-7324391-9-1

Part of the Tree Neutral® program, which offsets the number of trees consumed in the production and printing of this book by taking proactive steps, such as planting trees in direct proportion to the number of trees used: www.treeneutral.com

Printed in the United States of America on acid-free paper

20 21 22 23 24 25 . . . 0 9 8 7 6 5 4 3 2 1

First Edition

To my children Aidan, Jocelyn, and Robert.
To the American Humane board of directors, chaired by
John Payne, and most importantly, to the animals who
inspire us to build a more humane world.

# Table of Contents

# Foreword

"Leadership is the art of accomplishing more than the science of management says is possible."

—Colin Powell

A decade ago, the future of our nation's oldest animal welfare nonprofit, American Humane, was in doubt. The organization's storied history and rich legacy, like so many animals we help, had suffered from neglect.

Nonprofits and companies shutter their windows and close up shop all the time; that's the reality of a free and open market. In 2018, more than 20,000 businesses declared bankruptcy in the United States.[1] There is no safety net when an organization goes under. Jobs are lost, economies shrink, and everyone is worse off. For nonprofits that provide a social good, the constituencies they help are out of luck.

American Humane didn't avoid its financial crisis, but lived through it—not only surviving but thriving. The ship didn't miss the iceberg; it hit it head on and kept on chugging—bailing water while rebuilding the hull the whole time. At the helm of the ship was a leader who not only pulled together the finances and kept everyone on board but also ensured operational continuity when the waters were choppiest.

I've known Robin Ganzert for a decade. In that time, I've seen her transform American Humane, an organization with more than a century

---

1   https://www.uscourts.gov/news/2018/07/24/june-2018-bankruptcy-filings-fall-26-percent

of history, and put it on course for another 100 years of impact. I've had the opportunity to work alongside her as the chairman of the board at American Humane and have seen her in action.

The work American Humane does is important. For Robin, failure isn't an option—she isn't going to let down the animals and people who rely on American Humane. Robin uses all the management, financial, and leadership tools in her toolbox—and then some—to get the job done.

As an entrepreneur and an executive, I know how business works, what leads to profitability, and what leads to failure. There are few people I would trust to run a business for me, and among them is Robin. If you're a nonprofit leader or an executive at a for-profit company and you want to know the secrets for success, throw this book away. There are no shortcuts, and succeeding is never easy. As J. J. Watt, a defensive end for the Houston Texans, says, "Success isn't owned. It's leased, and rent is due every day."[2]

This book will give you the game plan on how to transform an organization on its last legs into a thriving operation, but you'll need the grit to get the job done.

—JOHN PAYNE, *chairman of the board*
*of American Humane, president and*
*CEO of Compassion-First Pet Hospitals*

---

2    http://www.espn.com/nfl/story/_/id/14155141/houston-texans-jj-watt-inspires-list-top-10-quotes
-andy-dalton-quip

# Getting the Job Done

"A Hurricane Warning is now in effect for #Florence from
South Santee River, South Carolina, to Duck, North Carolina,
including the Pamlico and Albemarle Sounds. Preparations
to protect life and property should be rushed to completion."

**—National Hurricane Center tweet September 11, 2018**[3]

The voice on the other end of the phone line was exhausted. "Robin," my director of rescue team operations asked, "do you know someone in North Carolina who has a truck?"

An American Humane Rescue truck, on its way to the Hurricane Florence impact zone, had broken down in Raleigh. Flooding from the hurricane had contaminated underground tanks of fuel in the surrounding area with water. After our American Humane truck filled up at a local gas station, its engine sputtered out, stopping the operation dead in its tracks.

It was a do-or-die situation. The truck was hauling boats that our American Humane Rescue team needed to traverse the floodwaters of Hurricane Florence. Either we could get the rescue boats to the impact zone and start saving animals, or we would fail in our mission to be first to serve whenever animals are in need. If we couldn't get our rescue boats there, we'd let down those we had promised to help.

In this situation, failure wasn't an option. So I turned to a constant source of support in my life—my mom. I reached for my phone.

"Mom," I said, "I need a truck. I've got a big trailer full of rescue boats in Raleigh. Can you help?"

"Well, Robin," my mother replied, "you know Scott, the man who shoes our horses? Scott will come."

I immediately got Scott, who was in Mocksville, North Carolina, on the phone. "Scott," I explained, "our rescue truck is stuck, and I need your help. It's already 5:30 PM, and we should already be in the water, rescuing animals. Can you help me?"

"I'll be there," Scott replied without hesitation. But then he asked, "Robin, I've got to take a meatloaf out of the oven. Can I do that first?"

"Absolutely," I said, "it may be your only hot meal for days. But if you drive through the night, then we're going to be able to start saving animals by morning."

When you're trusted with saving the lives of animals in danger, things can get hectic and tense. It requires a lot of grit and a lot of guts from our team members, full-time staff, volunteers, donors, and everyone in between to get the job done.

At the very heart of what we do, we are a humanitarian organization, the boots on the ground and first to serve all animals. We respond to the needs of animals whenever and wherever they are—whether they are caught up in a natural disaster and in need of rescue; on a movie set where they need protection; or in a farm, aquarium, or zoo where their welfare needs are not being met. That is where we lead, setting the standard and determining what it is to be humane. We act as the voice for the voiceless—rescuing, sheltering, protecting, and keeping animals safe from harm.

During Hurricane Florence, we were able to serve once again. Scott drove his own truck to Raleigh, where he picked up our truck and trailer at 9:30 PM. He drove it to the staging area where the rescue boats were being launched. By sun's light the next morning, our American Humane boats—with our volunteers and experts in water rescue—were in the floodwaters, saving lives.

Rescue is a 24-hour-a-day job, and it's not for the faint of heart. Frankly, some of the situations we find ourselves in can turn even the strongest stomachs, including my own. I sent my youngest rescuer, Amber, to help with our disaster response. Amber had responded to many disasters but none of this magnitude. She was trained for it, however, and felt in her heart of hearts she was ready for whatever was to come.

When a young person tells me they're ready to do this type of work, I believe them and send them into action. But I send them knowing they are going to be changed forever as a result of what they see, experience, and do. I always worry about compassion fatigue.

Amber got into the boat with our most experienced swift-water rescuer—our director of rescue operations—and they motored into the North Carolina floodwaters, not sure what they would find. As they approached a mobile home, they heard dogs barking. The home's porch was about four feet high, and it was completely underwater, and the inside of the home was four feet deep in dark, contaminated water. They waded into the flooded living room in their drysuits, where they found six pit bulls—all barking wildly, as if their lives depended on it. It was only when our team cautiously approached the frightened dogs that they figured out how some had managed to survive. The desperate animals were standing on the dead bodies of their littermates.

The team brought the surviving dogs onto our American Humane boats, which carried them to safety, to hope, and to compassion—an emotionally and physically draining undertaking and just one rescue among many.

It takes everyone giving their all to complete a successful rescue mission. It takes a farmer in North Carolina who gladly drove his own vehicle into harm's way to make sure our trucks and boats were able to complete their vital rescue missions. It takes the generous gift of prominent animal lovers like actress Victoria Principal, who donated the boats to American Humane. It takes the two rescue trucks we brought into North Carolina that were gifted to us by our dear friend and American Humane board member Lois Pope. It takes long-term relationships like those we built with the state of North Carolina officials to be able to deploy efficiently under appropriate disaster response protocols. And it takes compassionate people like our responders, who have the courage to see the most heartbreaking scenes and drop everything in their personal lives to deliver on the noble mission of humanitarian relief.

It's what we're all about. It's our *business*.

To fulfill our historic mission and to do so with integrity, we must take account of, evaluate, and know how to *run* our business. Our business is all about making a more humane world for people and animals. It's a business built on delivering social good. We appreciate that our responsibility as leaders in the humane movement and in the nonprofit sector requires a complete commitment to excellence in business, passion, and heart. Just as rescuing pit bulls from contaminated floodwaters is not for the faint of heart, neither was transforming an entire organization from top to bottom.

In 2010, I was invited to interview for the CEO position at American Humane by a recruiter who called and said, "We've been reviewing your background, and we thought this would be a terrific opportunity for you." The organization had already interviewed several candidates for the position, but I was intrigued.

At the time, I was deputy director of philanthropic services for the Pew Charitable Trusts in Washington, D.C.—one of America's premier nonprofit organizations. When I received the recruiter's call about the CEO position for American Humane, a national nonprofit known for its work with children and animals, I had already built a strong foundation in philanthropy and knew I was ready to take the next step with my career.

American Humane brought me in for an interview. I spoke with the interim CEO, a former American Humane board member who had been affiliated with the organization for a number of years. During our discussions about the position, he gave me a set of financials that were 18 months old, explaining they didn't have any more-recent reports. The financials showed that American Humane had a pattern of ongoing deficit spending. That was a little bit of a worry, but the interim CEO assured me the organization had $10 million in reserves.

I was offered and accepted the position. Little did I know that $10 million in reserves would be drawn down to just $1 million when I took the reins of American Humane 60 days later. That was just the first of many surprises.

It's been nearly a decade since I joined the team at American Humane. During that time, we've worked a lot of long, hard days and nights. Now, we're at a place where we're optimistic and excited about the future growth of our programs.

The results prove our efforts were worthwhile. Today, American Humane is proud of the following achievements:

- We rescue, shelter, feed, and protect nearly 1 billion animals each year.
- CharityWatch named American Humane a top-rated charity, with an A rating.
- We earned gold-level status with GuideStar USA.
- Charity Navigator, the country's top nonprofit watchdog, gave American Humane four stars, the highest of any major humane group.
- American Humane is one of fewer than one-tenth of 1 percent of US charities that made the Better Business Bureau's Wise Giving Alliance list.
- Ninety-one cents of every dollar spent goes directly into lifesaving programs, according to our fiscal year 2019 audit.
- Independent Charities of America awarded us their Seal of Excellence.
- We have been named a top-rated charity by Great Nonprofits.
- *Consumer Reports* called American Humane a best charity to support.

The past 10 years have taught me lessons—learned with blood, sweat, and tears—about the essentials of management in the charity space. Many of them were borrowed from the for-profit world, but all of them are essential to lasting success.

I've learned a lot about transformational leadership—rebuilding the boat while you're at sea. In the nonprofit world, there are two intricately linked ideas—mission and programmatic success. At its heart, that's what this book is about: defining your mission and achieving programmatic success.

In Chapter 2, I'll give you a brief overview of American Humane and the situation I inherited. It's a storied organization with over a century of history. We needed to look toward the future, however, not just reflect on the past. This chapter talks about what exactly constitutes transformational leadership and the parallels between for-profit businesses and nonprofits.

In Chapter 3, I'll discuss the starting point—building a crystal-clear mission at American Humane. All things flow from your mission; it's like the foundation of your house. You want a solid mission to rely on when things get shaken. There is a lot of work to be done after establishing the mission and before achieving the ultimate goal of programmatic success.

In Chapter 4, we'll explore building programs around the mission. At American Humane, we needed to evaluate our programs—their efficiency and how they related to the work for which we were chartered.

Then, in Chapter 5, we'll explain the necessity of hiring good leaders. Leaders are essential in any organization, whether for-profit or nonprofit. For example, our rescue team wouldn't be where it is today without the leadership of our director of rescue operations. His expertise is necessary whether rescuing pit bulls during Hurricane Florence or planning future missions.

In Chapter 6, we'll explore what culture looks like for any organization. Leaders give life and shape to the organization's culture every day. Culture is being ready to drop everything at the first sign of disaster and dive headfirst into rescuing animals.

Authentic brand and sound financials undergird all of our work. These are areas some don't like to talk about in the nonprofit space. They'd rather pretend that doing good work isn't reliant upon a sound marketing strategy or fundraising plan . . . both of which are essential components to programmatic success.

In Chapter 7, we'll consider how to build a brand that reflects the mission and emphasizes the work of the organization. Donors and volunteers are attracted by an authentic, candid brand. And, if you're in the nonprofit space, you can never have too many of either.

In Chapter 8, we'll look at structuring sound financials—making sure an organization can pay for its programs and people. We can't save, protect, and care for animals with only good intentions. Effective programs must pay for themselves. During Hurricane Florence, we needed donated rescue boats, trucks, food, and medical supplies. Although we use as much volunteer people power as we can, we still need hardworking, full-time staff managing the operation. You can't recruit and retain those people by paying them a pittance.

Lastly, in Chapter 9, we'll talk about what to do when your organization is out of the red and looking ahead. This is the story of how American Humane poised itself for the future.

During the past 10 years, we didn't tackle these things in a linear fashion but all at once. We got our financials under control while we were developing our brand, hiring smart leaders, refining our mission, building a culture, and executing programmatic success. Each is important—and each feeds into the other. You can't put these efforts on a flowchart, but you can group initiatives together and see how they support one another.

This book is a story of rebirth. It's a 10-year retrospective on working to save a nonprofit with more than a century of noble history and legacy. It serves as both a retelling of my time at American Humane and a how-to guide for nonprofit leaders interested in transformational leadership. Through reading this story, I hope you will glean insights into essential business practices that can transform any nonprofit and put it on the track to success. In each chapter, I'll explain how a key component of nonprofit success relates to our story—and other stories in both the nonprofit and for-profit spaces.

When you've finished this book, I hope you feel empowered to effect positive change in the world, whether you're leading a nationwide organization or looking to make an impact in your local community.

Let's get started.

## SAFETY TIPS FOR PETS DURING HURRICANE FLORENCE:
### Take Your Pets with You

Dr. Robin Ganzert's home, located in the barrier islands of South Carolina, was put under mandatory evacuation on Monday.

The owner of an 8-year-old Morkie (Maltese and Yorkie mix) named Daisy, Ganzert snapped photos of her pet, got her disaster prep kit ready—including a few toys for Daisy—and planned to head inland, away from the impact zone.

She is just one of the many pet owners whose homes are in the path of Hurricane Florence; however, she did something that experts advise every pet parent to do if they can: Get out early.

The dangerous storm is forecast to bring high winds, heavy rains and potential flooding to the coastal areas of South Carolina, North Carolina and Virginia over the coming days. Though it's a high-stress time for those living in the region, pet owners are encouraged to use this time to plan, prepare and stay informed.

"We recommend that all pet parents have a disaster kit on hand at all times," said Ganzert, CEO of American Humane, which has provided animal safety services for over 100 years.

Ganzert said pet owners should equip the kit for almost every situation by including items like a pet carrying case, food bowls, sanitation materials, chew toys, medication and veterinarian contact information.

Packing up-to-date photos of you and your pet can help provide additional proof of ownership or identification if you and your animal are separated.

"Last night I took some pix of Daisy, with her cute little summer haircut, so she's easily recognizable," Ganzert said.

Disaster kits don't have to be large, bulky plastic bins that may be difficult to travel with, experts say.

"You can even use a large Ziploc bag to pack everything," said Joe Elmore, CEO of Charleston Animal Society, a shelter within the evacuation zone. "Don't make it complicated. Stop by a local drug store. Get a human first-aid kit. Almost everything can be used if you or your pet has an emergency."

While packing food and water for both you and your pet may be one of the first things that comes to mind, it's easy to forget vaccination records or other relevant documents that could come in handy during an evacuation.

Without them, your pet may be put in quarantine at animal shelters or turned away altogether, Elmore said.

Most importantly of all, experts say, don't leave your pets home alone.

"Take your pets with you," said Elmore. "Don't just dump them at a shelter. Animal shelters are overwhelmed already. We're all overcrowded."

Ganzert said American Humane has relocated animals in the wake of Hurricane Florence. "During the middle of all of this, we were rescuing over 76 cats from an area that was going to flood in South Carolina—an area very prone to storm surges. These cats are now safely on the road, out of harm's way."

The felines are being moved to Connecticut and New York until the storm passes.

"We are working with shelters that are in the path of the hurricane to clear as many animals as we can so we can make room for pets that get displaced during the hurricane," said Kitty Block, CEO of Humane Society of the U.S.

Block, whose organization also assisted relief efforts during Hurricane Katrina, said thousands of people often choose not

*continued*

to evacuate because they fear leaving their pets behind. She said that the answer isn't showing up unannounced at an animal shelter but to instead call ahead.

For those who cannot evacuate, experts say choose a safe room in your home without windows to ride out the storm with your family and pets.

"They depend on you for food and water. Don't leave pets in vehicles," Ganzert said. She said to secure all exits in your home so your pets can't escape into the storm and to know your pet's hiding places because that's where they are likely to run.

The evacuation expert also warned against using tranquilizers during hazardous storms. "They'll need their survival instincts should the storm require that. They need to have all their wits about them," Ganzert said.

After the storm has passed, Ganzert said it's important to assess any damage before allowing pets to return home.

"Keep dogs on a leash and cats in a carrier," Ganzert said. "Displaced objects and fallen trees can disorient pets, and sharp debris could harm them."

Though there are precautions you can take, the best thing to do is get out of harm's way.

"People don't leave soon enough. People don't evacuate soon enough. It's better to be safe. People wait too long, and then it's too late," said Ganzert. "When your governor or your mayor says evacuate, please do like Daisy and I did."[4]

---

4   https://www.usatoday.com/story/news/2018/09/12/hurricane-florence-pet-safety-tips-experts/1271084002/

# A Tremendous Challenge

"Over the years, American Humane had settled for mediocrity rather than the relentless pursuit of excellence that separates the best national nonprofit institutions from the rest of the pack. Defining success, developing a laser-focused business mentality, and delivering programmatic excellence that furthers the mission will assure that American Humane will truly be the nation's voice."

**—Notes from the February 2011 CEO board report**

I started work on October 1, 2010. First on my agenda was to begin the transition with the interim CEO, who had agreed to stay on for three months. I met with him to determine where I should focus my attention during my first 30–90 days on the job. The interim CEO hung out every day at the office, bringing his little Yorkie with him to work. The office atmosphere was unusually casual and relaxed, and few seemed to have any urgency regarding operations, deliverables, or the financials. In fact, many of the local staff worked remotely, even though the office was located in a suburban community outside of Denver, where there wasn't much of a rush hour and commutes were not an issue.

Simply put, this culture was too relaxed. I would soon discover the interim CEO had given the executives, managers, and staff everything they requested in a bloated budget built on an unrealistic revenue projection. Everyone was understandably comfortable with the status quo, but this was a course for disaster. I was now at the helm of the ship with a $14 million deficit built into the fiscal year budget.

The work was just beginning, and I was soon so very grateful for my experience with nonprofit financial reporting. That's when I discovered that the promised $10 million rainy day fund had mostly been spent before I arrived. We were down to just $1 million when I walked in the door on my first day of work. The remaining funds were quickly evaporating at an unbelievable run rate that threatened bankruptcy in a matter of weeks.

I knew I was hired because of my strong track record in fundraising. That was no secret. It also became clear, however, the board wanted me to boost fundraising with the then-current program platform before I had a chance to even evaluate it. The key to long-term financial—and, ultimately, programmatic—success and sustainability is to ensure that every program is paying its own way with full costs covered. To ensure that happens, nonprofit programs need to be effective, efficient, relevant, and—particularly important—fundable.

The board didn't think there was any reason to waste my time reviewing American Humane's programs—they were convinced they were sitting on a gold mine that would generate plenty of support forever. At the time, there were a slew of programs broadly centered on two areas: saving animals and protecting children. They assumed these issues would always cause people to open their wallets and purses.

The global economy was still reeling from the aftereffects of the 2008–2009 Great Recession, and some nonprofits were hurting. The marketplace was picking winners and losers. For some reason, animal welfare groups were doing better at the time than organizations focused on child welfare. The child welfare units of many nonprofits were going out of business, and others were barely surviving on a shoestring. In fact, one of Chicago's oldest and strongest child welfare nonprofits was in the process of shutting its doors after being a powerhouse for decades.

Because American Humane had such a great mission and a dedicated team to support it, I was hopeful our organization might be among the winners. As I continued to look deeper into the organization's programs and financials, however, I began to wonder whether there was any hope of keeping the doors open.

Within 90 days of arriving on the scene, I completed an exhaustive, top-to-bottom review of every aspect of American Humane. I looked at programs, financials, employees, donors, vendor contracts, partner agreements, real estate, and everything else I could lay my eyes and hands on. My review turned up all sorts of landmines waiting to explode. I like to refer to these as "snakes in a can," and I just could not kick the can to the next generation of leaders at American Humane to solve—if there was a next generation of leaders at American Humane.

In addition to our near-empty coffers, the interim CEO had given American Humane's senior leadership team long-term employment contracts—again, locking the organization into financial commitments for years to come.

Our expenses weren't the only problem looming over the organization. When I reviewed our donor base, I found—much to my horror—a large gift to American Humane was $250. I had no major donors to go to for immediate support. There wasn't a Pew family sitting in the wings to provide an additional $10 million we so desperately needed.

I was tempted to reach out to my network and see if they had any job openings for me. But you can't walk out of a job 30 or 60 days after going into it. That's just not the right thing to do. I had no choice but to finish what I started and to test my resolve. I had to make it work no matter what. Our story is a case study in transformational leadership.

## THE POWER OF TRANSFORMATIONAL LEADERSHIP

More than 40 years ago, leadership expert James MacGregor Burns wrote, "Leadership is one of the most observed and least understood phenomena on Earth." This is clearly no longer the case. Although leadership is still one of the most observed phenomena on Earth, it is also one of the most understood. We know what makes great leaders tick, and we know how to help any leader become better and more effective.

Researchers have identified many different possible leadership styles: transactional, servant, and charismatic, just to name a few. In this instance, American Humane needed a very specific approach to management: transformational leadership. Eleanor Sullivan and Phillip Decker defined transformational leadership as "a leadership style focused on effecting revolutionary change in organizations through a commitment to the organization's vision." Typically, transformational leaders take the following actions:

- Create a vision of the future that will inspire and motivate an organization's employees, donors, and other stakeholders.

- Encourage a growth mindset that inspires employees to continuously develop their knowledge and skills.

- Achieve authenticity, are transparent, and communicate effectively—inside and outside the organization.[5]

- Encourage employees to be creative, to think outside the box, and to experiment with new things.

Transformational leaders have a tremendously positive effect on the organizations in which they work and on the people they lead. They don't just inspire and motivate the people who work for and with them; they help unleash much higher levels of performance. More specifically, according to a Concord Leadership Group report, people who work for transformational leaders—

- Are happier in their jobs and experience higher levels of well-being and positive mood. As a result, they are more committed to their organization.

---

5    https://concordleadershipgroup.com/!WakeUpCall_Report.pdf

- Are genuinely inspired by their leaders, who provide them with greater meaning in the completion of work-related tasks. This leads to enhanced individual and team productivity.

- Want to perform better because of a sense of being able to identify personally with the leader. They begin to define their own sense of success or failure in terms of the success or failure of the organization.

- Value the relationship they have with the leader because of the efforts the leader puts into employee development. This leads to higher levels of motivation and commitment.

- Build momentum behind an inspiring vision. The more compelling the vision, the greater the pride employees feel and the more time and effort they devote to serving the interests of the organization.

The good news is that any leader—whether they work for a for-profit or a nonprofit organization—can become a transformational leader. I have seen the power of transformational leadership in action, both in my previous organizations and at American Humane. At American Humane, we put together a remarkably effective team of leaders who transformed the organization for the better. Make no mistake about it: Transforming an organization, especially one that is large and well established, is an exhausting, all-consuming task. But I'm here to tell you it can be done.

To practice transformational leadership, you should do the following:

- Communicate a compelling vision of the future.

- Show and build respect within your team.

- Be a moral and ethical leader.

- Build pride in your team.

- Be confident and provide the members of your team with opportunities to build their own confidence.

- Discuss your organization's values with employees often.

- Instill a strong sense of purpose within your team.

- Solicit ideas and perspectives from all your people, and then really listen to what they have to say.

It's up to you to set the example for the behavior you want your people to engage in. When you do, they will follow.

## RUNNING A NONPROFIT LIKE A BUSINESS

In order to transform American Humane, we had to think about running a nonprofit like a regular business. That may seem counterintuitive, since for-profit businesses and nonprofit organizations have fundamentally different reasons for existing. For-profits exist to generate profit for their investors and owners, whereas nonprofits are focused on generating good social outcomes. Of course, in many cases, for-profits also want to generate good social outcomes. For example, Walmart operates the Walmart Foundation, which donated more than $1.4 billion in cash and in-kind gifts in 2016 to support its core areas of focus: opportunity, sustainability, and community.[6] However, for-profits are in business primarily to make money.

Although nonprofit organizations usually have different goals than for-profit businesses do, they do share many characteristics.

### Both exist to serve clients and customers

For-profits sell their products and services directly to consumers (for example, when you buy a Big Mac and fries at McDonald's), or they sell to other companies (when Coke sells its products directly to McDonald's, which then resells them to you). Nonprofits provide products and services to their "clients" and "customers"—often for free (when American Humane provides free veterinary services for animals in areas devastated by floods, hurricanes, tornadoes, and other natural disasters).

---

6    http://giving.walmart.com/our-focus

## Both need people to create, produce, and deliver products and services

Although for-profit and nonprofit organizations may have very different missions and goals, it takes people—employees, staff, leadership teams, boards—to operate effectively. Of course, talented people must be identified, recruited, hired, and developed in their jobs. This takes considerable time and money to accomplish.

## Both generate expenses

Although I don't believe there are many nonprofits that operate large manufacturing facilities such as those that produce Apple iPhones or General Motors automobiles, both types of organizations generate a variety of expenses as a natural consequence of regular operations. They must buy or rent office space and furniture; pay for computers, phones, copiers, and other office equipment; pay for electricity, Internet connections, and other utilities; pay salaries and sometimes bonuses—the list goes on and on.

## Both need an ongoing source of funds to conduct their operations

Because these organizations generate expenses, they need an ongoing source of funds. For-profit businesses get their funds from investors who buy shares of their stock (and thereby gain an ownership stake) and by selling their products and services. Nonprofits get their funds in the form of donations made by the general public, grants from private foundations and for-profit and other nonprofit organizations, and from the government.

Many of the kinds of things that businesses do, nonprofits do as well. As a result, nonprofits can become much more effective when they selectively adopt practices commonly used in business.

Leaders in many nonprofits are missing out on a tremendous opportunity to multiply and sustain their work when they rely on good intentions without leveraging the power of savvy business practices. When we applied good business practices at American Humane, it enabled the explosive growth we experienced in our programs and in the amount of revenue we're able to generate.

Let's look at some evidence. The Concord Leadership Group partnered with Bloomerang, Boardable, and DonorSearch to commission the Hartsook Centre for Sustainable Philanthropy at the University of Plymouth, UK, to conduct an in-depth study of nonprofit leadership in the United States. The results weren't pretty.

According to the study, 90 percent of nonprofit organizations engage in strategic planning. Within that group, 92 percent reported that their strategic plan was in writing, and 89 percent said that the plan had been reviewed and approved by the board.

The study showed, however, that just over half—55.8 percent—of the respondents indicated that staff members at all levels were involved in the planning process. This means that 4 in 10 strategic plans lack input from the employees expected to execute the work. In addition, only 47.4 percent of nonprofit leaders were assessed by the success or failure of the plan as a part of their annual performance appraisal—no accountability on top and no input from the bottom.[7]

There's an upside for improvement in many nonprofits today. If they improve participation in the strategic planning process and tie performance under the plan to the leaders who are charged with implementing it, organizational performance will surely improve. As a result, these nonprofits will have the ability to do more good in the world while delivering better outcomes.

Nonprofits have everything to gain and nothing to lose by applying basic but smart—yet sometimes difficult—for-profit business practices in their organizations. At American Humane, we take components we know succeed in the business world and apply them to the benefit of our animal and human stakeholders, who essentially serve as our shareholders. Our

---

7    https://concordleadershipgroup.com/!WakeUpCall_Report.pdf

shareholders, however, aren't investors looking at our market value or how much we have in liquid assets. Our shareholders are, in essence, the animals we rescue from disasters, the veterans who are paired with lifesaving service dogs, the animal actors who are protected during television and film productions, and so many more.

Our shareholders are also all the people across the country who donate precious resources to us so that we may protect the 9 billion farm animals who had no independently verified, science-based welfare protections before we came in; rescue and shelter the millions of animals who are abandoned every year; bring hope to the children with cancer whose hospital stays are brightened with the addition of a trained therapy animal; bring hope to the veterans who come back home from serving our country and struggle as they try to heal from the invisible wounds of war. Those are our shareholders, and that's where the real benefits and dividends accrue.

It's not just smart for nonprofits to apply the business practices of for-profits; there's a moral imperative to do so as well. One of our most sacred duties as nonprofit leaders is to properly steward donor contributions to effect social good. Our donors have entrusted us with their money, and we take that trust very seriously. I want to squeeze the most social good that we possibly can out of every single dollar we receive—to save the life of one more animal or to help one more veteran recover or to ensure that farm animals aren't mistreated.

Because we aren't a for-profit organization, we don't have a bottom line in the traditional sense; we look at surpluses or deficits in our financial statements, not profits or losses. One thing we do consider, however, is American Humane's triple bottom line: the social, economic, and environmental effects we are able to achieve.

## Social

We do a tremendous amount of social good out in the world every day of the week. It's what drives and motivates us to do what we do. We are fully committed to the animals, communities, and the world we serve.

## Economic

We are careful and effective stewards of the money donated to us, ensuring we can touch as many lives—both animal and human—as we possibly can.

## Environmental

We seek to create an improved, more humane environment for the billions of animals with which we share our planet. This is accomplished not only through programs that directly touch the lives of the animals themselves but also through national and international humane education campaigns intended to sensitize people to the challenges facing animals. It is critical we give people the tools to be kind to animals and to create a moral environment where animals are not mistreated but appreciated and loved.

I am extremely proud of our team. Together, we have built an organization that applies the best for-profit techniques effectively and efficiently to do tremendous social good across the United States and around the world.

If you want to improve the financial performance of your organization—whether it's a for-profit or nonprofit—get back to the basics. Ensure that your programs pay for themselves. Be frugal. Spend money only when needed. Create budgets and goals with your people and hold them accountable for achieving set targets. Track spending, and deal with variances as they arise, not next month or next year—or never. Reward employees who contribute to improving the financial performance of your organization and encourage them to keep raising the bar.

The process wasn't easy for us, and it won't be easy for you, but by breaking down the key components and looking for parallels in other nonprofits and businesses, our experience provides invaluable insights for nonprofit leaders interested in amplifying their own impact.

# VOICES FOR AMERICAN HUMANE
## LOIS POPE

Lois Pope is a longtime supporter and friend of American Humane who has served on the board of directors since 2012. Lois is one of America's leading philanthropists, and she has dedicated her life to helping those in need and improving the lives of the voiceless and vulnerable in our society. This stalwart mission is reflected in the three transformative organizations she has established: Leaders in Furthering Education (LIFE), the Lois Pope LIFE Foundation, and the Disabled Veterans' LIFE Memorial Foundation.

I asked Lois to tell us why American Humane is an important part of her life and what she sees for the future of the organization.

What I admire most about American Humane is that they are the true first responders in any emergency; they're first in—the first to serve. That's what's so important, because, ultimately, that is what saves lives. And that's what I'm mostly interested in: saving the lives of animals.

American Humane possesses what I call the three Cs: commitment, compassion, and competence. Each and every person who works there is a proof that it is possible to run an efficient organization while never losing one's soul and compassion. Simply put, they do an amazingly competent job in everything from rescues to education to putting on award shows and ensuring the safety of all creatures great and small.

Whenever I get involved with any organization, I hope to bring two assets. One is my willingness to give unfiltered advice based on years—way too many, I admit—of life experience. Two is financial. But I won't invest in anything unless I believe in its leadership, and I totally believe in Robin Ganzert. So, in addition to helping fund some of American Humane's most ambitious recent projects, my role is to give advice to Robin when asked and to serve as her sounding board when needed.

I think the key to the future of any organization, including mine, is to continue to develop new projects and new initiatives. Programs like Pups4Patriots™, where we find qualified dogs in need of forever homes and train them to become life-saving service dogs to help veterans with post-traumatic stress and traumatic brain injury. It's been my life's ambition and mission to help veterans. These dogs will lead the fight, and they will help bring them back while serving as companions to these brave men and women.

There are three lessons I believe any organization can learn from what American Humane has accomplished. Never lose sight of your brand and mission. Always look to creating new programs that connect with the modern audience; that's extremely important. And hire someone like Robin Ganzert.

# THREE EASY STEPS TO RUN A LEAN AND MEAN HUMANITARIAN ORGANIZATION: REFRESH, APPLY, AND COLLABORATE

The great recession is behind us, but its aftereffects can still be felt in the nonprofit sector. The economic downturn discouraged many donors from supporting humanitarian causes, forcing nonprofit organizations to cut programs, reduce salaries (or eliminate staff altogether), and delay paying vendors for services.

Nearly a decade later, many nonprofits are still racking up massive deficits. Since 2008, the sector has been running deficits 4 percent to 8 percent of its total revenue each year.

I saw it firsthand. When I joined American Humane in 2010, the organization operated at a multimillion-dollar deficit during each of the previous four years.

But it's not a death sentence. To run a successful humanitarian organization, you have to worry about two bottom lines: social ROI and financial ROI. Your donors want to know that their money isn't being wasted, but they also want to see the organization creating positive change in the world through effective programs. It's not enough to represent an "honorable cause"—donors want a tangible return on their charitable gift.

Here's how you can give it to them:

## Refresh your programs

Don't just keep doing something because it has always been done that way—especially if it's expensive. Take the time to re-evaluate your programs. Conduct an internal review. Poll your donors (or the general public) to gauge the popularity and effectiveness of a program. I recommend a listening tour, where you meet with industry leaders to understand just how well the program is received outside your office. For our organization, I once embarked on a year-long listening tour to develop a new funding model for an outdated program. Based on suggestions from industry leaders, I was able to brainstorm new processes and, in the end, secure approval for the new funding model.

Before changing anything, simply taking the time to listen can pay huge dividends down the road.

## Apply the "Jack Welch mentality" to evaluate those programs

A nonprofit CEO has to have the heart and the smarts. That requires a critical eye to objectively assess effective and ineffective programs. As former General Electric CEO Jack Welch once said, "Face reality as it is, not as it was or as you wish it to be."

Ask yourself: Are your programs giving you the best bang for the buck? Are they leaders (or close seconds) in the field? What differentiates you? Can you narrow your platform to play to your strengths? What is the financial ROI? Social ROI? These questions might seem onerous but answering them will help you refocus your energy and resources on what your organization does best.

We had 40 disorganized programs when I first started. Now we have four platforms, each of which leads its field. The organized structure increases our operating efficiency and capacity to analyze results. This takes patience—structural reform never happens overnight.

## Collaborate with organizations that share a common interest

Humanitarianism is a lot easier when there's collaboration between organizations. You can pool brainpower and resources to get more done, while simultaneously generating publicity for your cause. For example, we partner with local pet stores to raise money to provide lifesaving service dogs to veterans suffering from post-traumatic stress. In November 2018, we partnered with the National Football League's New York Giants to sponsor a surprise gift of a trained PTS service dog, presented to a military veteran during a Giants game against the Philadelphia Eagles at MetLife Stadium.

Partnerships between nonprofits are just as valuable. They not only produce tangible results but foster a healthy exchange of information between organizations. So find a partner and get out there![8]

---

8    https://www.forbes.com/sites/forbesnonprofitcouncil/2017/02/06/three-easy-steps-to-run-a
     -lean-mean-humanitarian-organization/#7d19ce9be2dd

# Positioning for Operational Success

"Mission is the star we steer by. Everything begins with mission; everything flows from mission."

**—Frances Hesselbein, former CEO of the Girl Scouts**

For nonprofits, mission comes before everything else. Out of your mission flow your programs, finances, hiring decisions, and culture. It's the cornerstone upon which organizations build successful operations.

I say *organization* because while mission is important at both for-profit and nonprofit enterprises, it's essential for nonprofits. Nonprofits exist to fulfill a specific purpose rather than just to generate revenue. Mission, then, is inextricably tied with functioning well in the nonprofit space.

What makes a good mission? Missions should be crystal clear and easily digestible. They need to influence every level of management, every decision, and every action of the organization. Every employee, from a new hire to senior leadership, should be able to articulate how their job contributes to the overarching mission.

Let's say you run a nonprofit that wants to increase access to healthy food. All of your programs should be focused on achieving that goal. Your mission informs how you operate: Are you buying food or growing it? Are you cooking it yourself or outsourcing that labor? Are you selling food at an affordable rate, or are you giving it away? The answer to each question lies within your mission and how you can most efficiently fulfill your organization's purpose.

At American Humane, our mission is to build a more humane world. But that goal can encompass a lot. To exacerbate the matter, American Humane was founded in 1877. The world has changed a lot in the last 140-plus years. Our mission is timeless, but when I arrived at American Humane, how we contrived to implement it was muddled and inefficient. In other words, as we had grown and adapted over more than a century of work, we had let our organization become increasingly susceptible to mission drift. Mission drift—when an organization moves away from its mission, either consciously or unconsciously—can plague any organization, not just nonprofits. As a result, every organization must be ever vigilant in the face of mission drift, constantly evaluating the decisions they make. Even good-intentioned decisions can result in mission drift.

Consider a story relayed in the *Harvard Business Review*. A nonprofit job-training agency was tasked with the mission of preparing students to work in the culinary arts. To further this mission, they decided to invest in a large, industrial kitchen. Out of this kitchen, they would run a restaurant, a catering service, and a wholesale food company. These enterprises would give students hands-on work experience that would prepare them for jobs in the culinary world. As a bonus, the nonprofit would generate additional income that could be used to fund other programs.

Donors were excited by the promise of the program and eagerly poured money into the construction of the kitchen. But the kitchen and its operations quickly became a millstone around the nonprofit's neck. Combined, the three enterprises lost a quarter of a million dollars every year. The programmatic reward for this gargantuan money sink was minimal—just 10 students were finding jobs every year as a result of the program. In terms of their mission, they were paying roughly $25,000 for each student to find a job.[9]

---

9   https://hbr.org/2005/02/should-nonprofits-seek-profits

This is an example of how pursuing earned income can lead to mission drift for a nonprofit. Maybe opening a kitchen could be a great idea for our hypothetical nonprofit that wants to increase access to food but here, it just didn't make sense. Nonprofits that try to establish revenue-generating operations can quickly find themselves sucked into a corporate nightmare.

Most academics who analyze mission drift focus on finances as a primary culprit. As any leader knows, funding is essential for an organization—the lights need to be on if you want to help people, so your mission must be able to attract donations, but seeking revenue shouldn't overshadow the work itself. Pivoting to earned-income programs—or taking on substantial government contracts—often leads to mission drift as your programs reorient around new sources of revenue.

If our hypothetical food access nonprofit took on a government contract to dispense food to low-income households, that contract could become their entire purpose. They would be distributing food for the government and would become reliant on the funding for that program. Soon, the organization could become merely an extension of the government, and all of the decisions made by the leadership team would be about maintaining that contract.

Relying on one source of funding is tricky, as anyone involved with the for-profit business world will tell you. Consider Makin Bacon, the invention of an 8-year-old girl—Abbey Fleck—and her father, Jon. The duo created a bowl with three bars to hang bacon on, so that when you microwaved the bacon, the fat dripped off and the meat didn't become soggy. The family sold their product primarily through *Good Housekeeping* magazine and received orders directly.

Then, business exploded when Walmart ordered 200,000 Makin Bacon dishes to sell. Immediately, Walmart became the primary source of income for the Fleck family's fledgling business. With the increase in sales came an increase in liability. Since Walmart was their largest buyer, if the company ever decided to drop them, they would likely go out of business—stuck with far too much of their product that they would have difficulty selling via other channels.[10] Luckily, nothing cataclysmic like that ever happened, and with the rapid expansion of Amazon, the Fleck family has another channel through which to sell their product.[11]

Pursuing monolithic funding sources is just one example of how mission drift can manifest. When I arrived at American Humane, I quickly realized that mission drift hadn't crept in from one direction but from all sides. We had some serious disconnects when it came to our mission and the work we were doing.

Our focus was too wide, and the scope of our work was overly broad. As an organization, we were spread too thin, advocating for both animals and children on a myriad of fronts. Although much of the work we were doing for animals was uniquely our own—like Humane Hollywood—a great deal of the work we were doing on behalf of children was not uniquely ours and, frankly, being done better by other organizations that focus solely on children. In truth, even some of our work on behalf of animals had wandered far away from the core mission of American Humane. We were the poster child for mission drift.

I'd been hired to revamp the organization's finances, but I knew that reestablishing our mission and focus were among my highest priorities. Aside from mitigating the damage from mission drift, I recognized that clarity of focus has quantifiable benefits.

Consider the results of a Deloitte survey of more than 1,000 people at organizations with at least 100 employees. They found overwhelming evidence that purpose-driven organizations thrive. More than 8 in 10 people working at an organization with a strong sense of purpose were confident their organization would grow in the coming year, whereas 50 percent of the employees at organizations without purpose were doubtful that their organization would grow. Purpose leads directly to optimism, commitment, and engagement.

---

10   https://www.chron.com/life/books/article/The-Wal-Mart-Effect-by-Charles-Fishman-1859885.php
11   https://makinbacon.com/about.php

In the nonprofit space, you need employees who are committed to the cause. I knew that, with a well-defined mission, I could reenergize our employees and set us on the track for success.[12] We needed a vision for the future.

Referring to Microsoft, the company he founded, Bill Gates once famously said, "Innovate or die." With so much change going on in the world today, and everything moving faster than ever before, if an organization is standing still, it's falling behind. Stand still long enough, and even the most successful companies will falter. Just ask the men and women who ran Kodak, Blockbuster, or Nokia. These companies were all wildly successful in their prime, but they failed when they couldn't adapt as the world changed around them.

I didn't want American Humane to become the Blockbuster of the nonprofit space. After all, we had changed, but not in ways that aligned with our founding mission. We needed to reorient ourselves and prepare for the future.

The world that American Humane occupied when I took charge as CEO was evolving at a fast pace, and it was becoming a more hostile environment for nonprofits. The era was marked by compassion fatigue, which made positioning American Humane to be relevant, timely, and timeless in the delivery of our mission even more important. As I explained in the foreword of our 2011 annual report,

> **Compassion fatigue has impacted American communities, as the constant stream of headlines about mounting unemployment, unstable financial markets, and political strife continue to pressure-test our mettle and challenge our resolve. Rising rates of abuse and neglect are being met by a lack of community solutions, compounded by**

---

12  https://www2.deloitte.com/content/dam/Deloitte/us/Documents/about-deloitte/us-leadership
    -2014-core-beliefs-culture-survey-040414.pdf

> a lack of funding . . . Today, the issues impacting our
> communities have dramatically affected our children
> and animals, and brought even more barriers to building
> social capital, family engagement, and pet ownership.

Although the ultimate decisions about the future direction of American Humane would need the support and approval of the board, it was my job to give them my best recommendations, strategies, and plans. And that's exactly what I set about to do. Completing a successful turnaround of the organization was going to require a lot of creativity and a lot of energy. It wasn't simply a revenue problem; it was much deeper than that. There had been so much going on in terms of mission drift and a lack of performance by the staff members to deliver on a mission. And it wasn't all their fault, because there wasn't any clear strategic direction from the top.

What was going to be our direction, or as Frances Hesselbein would ask, what would be our mission star? We needed to focus on our roots to see where our organization could grow.

To that end, in 2010, with funding from Zoetis, the world's largest animal health company, we launched the Canines and Childhood Cancer Study to rigorously measure the effects of animal-assisted therapy on children with cancer, their parents, and therapy dogs. That study cut to the core of who we are—measuring the importance of the magnificent bond between people and animals.

It progressed to a full clinical trial at five different sites across the country that lasted more than two years. Children in the treatment group received 20-minute sessions with a therapy dog about once a week for four months, in addition to their standard care.

The results of the study, published in the *Journal of Pediatric Oncology Nursing*, were as remarkable as they were uplifting. The study clearly showed that regular visits from a therapy dog can provide significant psychosocial benefits to families of children undergoing treatment for cancer. The data indicated positive effects on parents, including improved communication within families as well as between parents and medical staff, which can lead to better medical care and reductions in their levels of stress, specifically as it relates to their emotional functioning.

One of the sites for the clinical trial was the Children's Hospital at Vanderbilt, in Nashville, Tennessee. There, pet therapist Michelle Thompson and her specially trained toy Pomeranian, Swoosh, participated in therapy sessions with children who had been diagnosed with cancer.

According to the father of Bryce Greenwell, a patient diagnosed with acute lymphoblastic leukemia, "It gave us something to talk about, to take his focus off what was really happening. It wasn't all about the needles and pokes and prods. For Bryce, Swoosh was something to look forward to. He could hang out with Swoosh for a little bit."

Adds Bryce's mother, "Bryce would have to take an antianxiety medication prior to many clinic appointments to ease his anxiety. But when he saw Swoosh, his anxiety level went down without the use of medicine. It was a little light into the nightmare that we were living."

Amy McCullough, PhD, principal investigator of the study and American Humane's national director of humane research at the time, said, "This study advances our understanding of the benefits of the vital bond shared between people and animals. We believe the findings may further increase access to therapy animals in hospital environments, enhance therapy dog training and practice, and improve well-being outcomes for families facing the challenges of childhood cancer."

After years of anecdotal evidence pointing to the benefits of animal-assisted therapy on families of children with cancer, we were finally able to examine in a rigorous manner the scientific underpinning of its effectiveness. We created the first and the largest clinical trial that's ever been done to show the benefits of animal-assisted interaction for kids with cancer. And with more than 10,000 children diagnosed with cancer each year, the widespread use of therapy dogs in a treatment setting could have a profoundly positive impact on the lives of many.

That study encapsulates, in a lot of ways, what American Humane is all about and helped further refine our mission. Today, our mission statement is bold, clear, and actionable:

*OUR MISSION*

**American Humane is committed to ensuring the
safety, welfare, and well-being of animals.**

If you know much about American Humane, you may notice that children are no longer part of our mission. That was a tough decision and one that will be explained in further detail when we dig deeper into our programs in the upcoming chapters. We didn't home in on our mission immediately but refined it over time while we rehashed our programs, leadership, finances, and culture.

Now, our mission guides everything we do. At any nonprofit, that's how a mission should function.

## KEY TAKEAWAYS

- Every organization needs a clear and compelling mission—a star to steer by. The mission provides the vehicle to align the actions of employees with the goals of the organization.

- Combat mission drift at every turn. If you're a nonprofit, is pursuing earned income worth it? Will it come at the expense of your mission?

# VOICES FOR ANIMAL HUMANE
## CANDY SPELLING

Candy Spelling has served on the American Humane board of directors since 2012—she is currently the vice chair. Candy is a best-selling author, columnist, Broadway producer, and star of the record-breaking HGTV series *Selling Spelling Manor*. She was married to Hollywood producer Aaron Spelling from 1968 until he passed away in 2006.

Candy is perhaps most well known for her philanthropy. She has freely given her time to a variety of civic and charitable activities, including serving on the boards of the UCLA Health System and LA's Best—an after-school enrichment program that serves in-need children through partnerships with the Los Angeles Unified School District, the City of Los Angeles, and the private sector.

I asked Candy to tell us why she is such an enthusiastic supporter of American Humane and what the organization means to her.

> When I first learned about American Humane years ago, it was the gold standard of organizations established to ensure the welfare and safety of animals. But, more importantly, I saw that they were pursuing their mission in a really hands-on way. They were literally getting out in the field to make the lives of animals better, whether it was during a time of crisis or matching dogs up with military veterans or working to strengthen the bonds between animals and people. The work of American Humane also touches people—children and adults—and not only the animals. They improve the lives of every animal and every person they work with.
>
> I believe that, in the vast majority of cases, American Humane's programs have a twofold purpose. First, they make the lives of animals better, which is core to the organization's mission. Second, they educate the public in important animal-related topics. The milestone No Animals Were Harmed program for the television and film industries, which ensures that the animals used in storytelling by the creative community will be protected, is a good example of this. No Animals Were Harmed clearly makes the lives of animals safer and better, and it has for many years now. But I also believe

that the program has had an enormous impact over many years in raising everyone's awareness about the welfare of animals. The program continues today and is truly unmatched in its reach.

The American Humane team is smart, prepared, and ready to turn on a dime. They see a problem and they jump in and do whatever it takes to solve it. For example, I was able to watch the tireless efforts of the American Humane team and board member Lois Pope change US government policy that prohibited military veterans from adopting the dogs they worked with overseas, often in combat. I flew to Washington, D.C., twice to be a part of this effort—helping to raise awareness about the issue and meeting with members of Congress on Capitol Hill. We were successful in strengthening the law to ensure that military working dogs be brought back home to the United States when they retire and that the first right of adoption be granted to their military handlers and their families.

Another time the American Humane team really impressed me was in 2013, after the devastating tornadoes that hit Moore, Oklahoma, killing 24 people and injuring hundreds of others. I attended the Healing in the Heartland benefit concert in Oklahoma City, where Miranda Lambert's vulnerable performance of "The House That Built Me" [moved] the crowd, including me. Everyone was in tears.

The slideshow projected behind Miranda highlighted the emergency rescue efforts of the American Humane Rescue team that mobilized just days after the May 20 tornadoes hit. With the help of Miranda Lambert and her MuttNation Foundation, Red Star, now called American Humane Rescue, was invited to the state of Oklahoma as an approved first responder to help provide emergency rescue operations, sheltering, and much-needed care for animals injured or separated from their owners. When disasters hit, our rescue trucks are there.

# Operating with Clarity

"In the business world, the rearview mirror is always clearer than the windshield."

**—Warren Buffett**

When I took the helm as CEO, American Humane operated 40 different programs and a staff of 140. Some were disconnected. Some overlapped. None covered their full costs. Many operated without a single funding source. They weren't all aligned to the same mission. As I explained earlier, getting our mission into shape moved in tandem with restructuring everything else. As a result, rethinking our programs gave us insight into our mission.

I had learned well from previous experience that no organization—whether for-profit or nonprofit—can thrive and grow if its programs don't pay for themselves. Eventually, the reckoning day comes. Deficits get approved, losses are written off, cash gets tight, salaries and bills don't get paid, and the organization is shut down. In the case of a for-profit business, this usually results in bankruptcy. In the case of a nonprofit, donors are left wondering where their contributions had been going all those years, and the constituencies you're supposed to help are left out in the cold.

Change never comes quickly enough, it's never as enduring as anyone would wish, and it never comes on its own. We didn't have the luxury of investing in programs that did not represent a center of excellence and that did not remove the threats to the well-being of the animals and children we were committed to protecting. In short, if we weren't doing the best job possible for these two constituencies, then we would have to either invest more money, time, and other resources into them to raise the bar considerably, or let them go.

If your mission says you're supposed to help children and animals, you'd better be certain that your programs are accomplishing just that.

## WHICH PROGRAMS TO KEEP AND WHICH TO CUT?

Soon after I arrived at American Humane, I learned that the children's welfare team had a large convention scheduled in just a couple of weeks. They said, "You need to come see us in action," and I agreed that would be a good idea; it was part of my fact-finding efforts.

I have been to many wonderful conferences over the years—all around the world. When I arrived at this conference, however, I realized that something was not right. The sessions were poorly attended; there were only four or five people in a room listening to the research presentations.

I knew we were pouring millions of dollars into our children's welfare program, but if this was the end result in terms of interest and impact, why was this program still such a large part of our staffing and budget? It just didn't add up. So we embarked on an in-depth analysis of our programs. The fundamental questions were these: Which current programs should we keep, which should we drop, and which emerging programs should we consider adding to our roster?

Strategic program investment was essential to the future success and financial viability of American Humane. Our program environment was fragmented. We were trying to do too much with too little and, as a result, our most important and successful programs suffered from the lack of investment. In short, our less-effective programs were dragging down our mission-focused programs and putting them and our organization in danger.

How exactly could we decide which existing programs to drop and which new programs to take on? This required taking a different approach than had been done in the past. It required unlearning the old ways of doing things and learning new ways of doing things. Instead of using emotion or the comfort of the status quo or the laurels of our past successes to determine which programs we should focus our resources on, we would need to look at our organization like a business—using the tools that businesses use to determine their focus.

We were also looking for what made us different from other humane nonprofits. The humane landscape had grown very crowded. Suddenly, local humane organizations, shelters, and rescue groups were growing by leaps and bounds across our great country. Everybody loved animals, everybody had *always* loved animals, but the trend was toward greater involvement with local shelters and rescue groups. As a national organization, this made figuring out our differentiators and competitive advantages critically important.

Our program analysis used the kind of fundamental techniques that most any business or MBA student would be familiar with but that get lost among emotion-filled words in many nonprofit organizations: saving animals, saving children, saving the world. We were doing it all, but no one had gone back to the basics of business to analyze the effectiveness of our programs and whether they were paying their way.

We conducted a standard SWOT analysis (a 2 × 2 matrix that looks at the strengths and weaknesses internal to the organization and the opportunities and threats external to the organization). It's not cool or new, but it was new for us.

To get a better idea about the viability of our programs—particularly, our child welfare program—I brought in a child welfare expert. I wanted to see whether our programs had any relevance in a very crowded and complicated space. I also asked her to go through every single one of our existing child welfare programs to answer these questions: Are we a leader in this space? Are we in the top three?

In fact, in every single one of those areas, we were not a leader. We were not in the top three. In most of those areas, we weren't even a top-10 provider as recognized by the external expert community. We were a historic provider, but we were not now a leader in any of those areas. That old shine had worn off, and other incredible organizations had taken on that work and seized the leadership momentum around child welfare.

Then, I did a further test to see if the child welfare work was fundable. We did beautiful direct-mail pieces for both children and animals and sent them out, asking for donations around these two areas. The direct-mail piece for children raised a total of only about $76. The direct-mail piece for animals, however, raised considerably more—about $9,000. We could clearly see that the child welfare work did not resonate with our donors.

Despite all the resources we were devoting to it and all the emotional attachment it had organizationally, the child welfare platform was not one of American Humane's crown jewels. It wasn't funded, it wasn't fundable, and we were not ranked as any sort of leader in the space. We were diverting critical institutional resources to an area that wasn't successful for us.

I pointed out to the board that American Humane could achieve significant national impact if the organization refocused its resources on two specific program areas:

- Our crown jewel marquee programs, such as our familiar No Animals Were Harmed program and American Humane Rescue.
- Programs that offered substantial potential for helping the largest number of animals, such as the American Humane Certified™ farm animal welfare program and Animal-Assisted Therapy.

My plan to focus on these two areas and set aside the other legacy programs encountered understandable resistance. Each board member had legacy programs that they supported, and these programs were often the reason they had joined the board in the first place. So it was no surprise to me that there would be resistance to changes in our programmatic structure.

The greatest resistance came from the hard decision to give up our children's program platform. This program was a key part of American Humane's legacy. Child safety and protection had been part of our agenda from the very beginning, and in 1883, we supported the passage of the first Cruelty to Children Act. Other excellent nonprofits had stepped up to focus their own efforts on doing incredibly important work in the area of child welfare. Our work was important, and we were doing good things, but it wasn't achieving the degree of external recognition and funding required to make it something we could or should continue to invest in. And by competing for resources with other programs that were getting the job done, we weren't optimizing the help our key constituencies should be receiving.

Of course when we started rolling out these new ideas to our staff, we encountered the greatest resistance. They realized that it was a new day for accountability and performance, which understandably made most everyone nervous, frightened, and anxious. As I conducted town halls with our employees, it was, for many, the first time they saw institutional numbers—the deficits we had been incurring for years. It was the first time they saw what it would take to bring in the revenue required day to day to keep American Humane open and viable. It was the first time they saw the entire disclosure across the institution from a historical standpoint, where we were at the time, and where we had to go looking forward. I knew I needed to build consensus within the organization to make the necessary changes, but to do that, everyone needed to understand what we were all facing together.

It wasn't just me as the new CEO who was facing this; it was all of us on the American Humane team facing it. We had the advantage that members of our staff were deeply committed to our work. But how were we going to bring everyone together to understand that we had to solve the organization's problems together? We had a revenue problem, an expense problem, a mission problem, and a cultural problem. There were many problems to be solved, and we would have to do it together.

We decided to move ahead with the focus on promoting our crown jewels, which included these programs:

- No Animals Were Harmed®—our marquee certification program that monitors animals working on film and TV lots and sets around the world.

- American Humane Rescue™—our core program of animal rescue, which responds to the needs of animals in emergencies, including natural disasters.

- The Second Chance® Fund—financial assistance to help offset the costs of rescuing animals who are homeless or the victims of human cruelty.

The emerging programs offering the greatest potential for the organization at the time included the following:

- American Humane Certified farm animal welfare

- Animal-Assisted Therapy

- The Front Porch Project™—a national child abuse prevention program, educating and training members of the community to be eyes and ears for kids in need

These were the proven programs with market appeal. We then identified where we could have a significant impact if we made disciplined investments in those programs to be successful. That was our first step.

As I explained in my first report to the board, a handful of our historical legacy programs (Be Kind to Animals Week®, Adopt-A-Cat Month®, Adopt-A-Dog Month®) had market potential but would require in-depth reviews to define success, institutional branding, and meaningful impact. We could potentially leverage our corporate and celebrity partners to revive these initiatives, but there were no guarantees. Every program would need to become sustainable, funded, fundable, marketable, relevant, reliable, timely, and timeless if we were to survive as an organization.

Based on our review of finances, social ROI, reputation capital, and other factors, we took our hodgepodge of 40 different programs and focused them down to just four distinct (and distinctive) program planks that were all aligned toward the same mission. These became the guiding coordinates on the American Humane roadmap, and it enabled us to align our people with our work.

## Humane Intervention—Rescue

Through the Humane Intervention—Rescue program, we work in association with America's first responders, civic leaders, animal-protection advocates, healthcare providers, and families to prepare for and cope when crises and disasters strike. Its key initiatives include Rescue Services, which responds to the needs of animals in emergencies; Animal-Assisted Therapy; and the Second Chance Fund for Animals.

## Humane Research and Policy Solutions

Working in association with American policymakers, thought leaders, scientists, and the public, the Humane Research and Policy Solutions program builds enduring solutions to the most pressing challenges facing children and animals. Its key initiatives include supporting the Animal Welfare Research Institute, articulating a clear legislative agenda, and advocating for humane policies.

## Humane Heartland—Healthy Animals, Healthy Kids

The Humane Heartland program works in association with American farmers, ranchers, animal advocates, veterinarians, academics, distributors, consumers, and communities to enhance the welfare of farm animals and the health and well-being of children, families, and communities. Its key initiatives include the American Humane Certified farm welfare certification program and national educational efforts promoting humane food choices.

## Humane Hollywood

Finally, the Humane Hollywood program, working in association with the American film and TV industries, ensures the well-being of animal actors and promotes the human–animal bond. Its key initiatives are the No Animals Were Harmed certification program for film and television productions, the American Humane Hero Dog Awards®, which airs on Hallmark Channel, and celebrity outreach to gain a wider national voice for the voiceless.

Our four focused themes were thoroughly market tested with key constituents in New York and Florida before we presented them to the board. The feedback we received was overwhelmingly positive. One constituent involved in the market test said she had goose bumps when she read the new themes for the first time. Another constituent remarked that the new themes harkened back to American Humane's glory days a century before. Without a doubt, they transformed a disparate, disjointed program platform while positioning American Humane for success. The new program planks clearly set forth where we would focus our efforts as an organization while providing four well-defined areas for which we could measure outcomes.

One year after my first board meeting, American Humane had a rudder again: these four guiding coordinates for how we were going to define our work moving forward. If our current work didn't fall within one of our new program planks, then we would drop it. And if our proposed new work didn't fit, then we wouldn't pursue it. Our focus would be only on programs within the four planks. Focus. Focus. Focus.

I can remember when I unveiled the new program planks to our board. I had them blown up on large displays. I'm pretty sure that everyone in the room felt a sense of relief and thought, "Finally, this is who we are." Up until then, our mission was so broad and our programs so disjointed, that no one really knew what we did, what our focus was.

We successfully completed the most transformative exercise in American Humane history. We completely redefined our historic organization's mission and our program platforms. We renewed or revived the lifesaving legacy programs that were on track to go under and disappear. We eliminated mission drift. We did this all in less than a year.

## HUMANE HOLLYWOOD—A CASE IN POINT

One of our most well-known marquee programs is Humane Hollywood. Anyone who has ever watched a film or television show with animal actors is surely familiar with the famous words in the end credits, "No Animals Were Harmed." What few knew, however, is that even this marquee program was in trouble when I took charge of American Humane. The funding for our program to protect animal actors in films and television had not been increased for many years, while the scope of work had grown by leaps and bounds.

In the early decades of Hollywood filmmaking, most filming was done in studios and on studio lots in the Los Angeles area. This made monitoring the use of animal actors in films easier and less expensive, because most productions were done within a relatively small geographic area. The advent of new technologies over the past couple of decades allowed people to start shooting films throughout the country and all around the world—sometimes using the Internet or high-definition cameras that cost very little. As a result, we suddenly found our services were more in demand than ever, and the same level of funding we used for our studio model in the 1960s and 1970s just wasn't enough. We actually ended up paying money out of our own pocket to keep our dedicated Certified Animal Safety Representatives on the set, to read through the scripts, to anticipate problems, to monitor the animal action on the sets, and to do all the other things that keep animals safe. Their work helps make sure some 100,000 animals working on more than 1,000 sets around the world are kept safe and are treated humanely.

Having defined our new program platforms, we were now able to build and rebuild the future business models for our four key areas, including the Humane Hollywood program.

We installed new professional leadership at the top of every program plank. We invested in professional development and training. We invested in public awareness and external communications. Importantly, we also measured outcomes for all program deliverables and held leadership accountable to the strategic plan.

For the new Humane Hollywood business model, a new chief veterinary officer was onboarded—the first medical professional to oversee this prestigious program. More than 30 percent of the workforce was remade to include licensed veterinarians as our frontline safety monitors, stationed in high-production areas for film and television studios and sets around the world. Just as important, the funding model needed to be revamped. After intensive meetings with industry leaders, funding sources were adequately provided to allow for this program to stand on its own for the first time in more than 30 years. Based on its success, we implemented program-specific variations of this model in all our divisions.

The result was a more than 2,000 percent increase in the number of animals helped—from 50 million to 1 billion each year! That is a real and measurable return on investment for our mission.

## KEY TAKEAWAYS

- If a program (or product, in the case of a for-profit organization) can't pay for itself, then either invest more money, time, or other resources to make it viable, or let it go.

- Use fundamental business tools, such as SWOT analysis, to determine where you should focus your attention and resources.

## Reuniting America's battle buddies:
### *The story of Matty and Brent*

Staying true to your mission while innovating new solutions is the lesson that can be learned from the story of two best friends who each thought they had lost the other until, with a little help, their special connection was found once more.

Retired Army Specialist Brent Grommet and Military Working Dog Matty, a Czech German shepherd, developed an unbreakable bond while stationed together in Afghanistan, serving our country as a bomb-detection team. Using his superhuman sense of smell, Matty directed his human handler to hidden IEDs (improvised explosive devices), working day and night to protect our military troops from the deadly bombs.

Specialist Grommet says Matty saved his life and the lives of everyone in his unit more than once. One day, they were searching a bazaar for IEDs when their unit walked into an ambush. During the firefight, they took casualties. Matty and Brent raced to clear a helicopter landing zone of IEDs while taking direct mortar fire.

After they got their wounded out, Matty and Brent went back to the front line and were engaging the enemy when they were hit with a rocket-propelled grenade, knocking both of them unconscious and giving Brent a traumatic brain injury—one of several injuries the pair suffered together. Finally, Matty and Brent were driving in a truck that was hit by two roadside bombs. They were flown back to the United States for treatment. Although Brent had already filled out adoption paperwork for his canine companion, while he was having neurosurgery, unbelievably enough, Matty was wrongly given to someone else. The two friends lost track of each other. Soldier and dog were separated, but the handler never gave up the search for his companion, despite running into numerous dead ends and frustrating bureaucratic stonewalling.

*continued*

Brent's dad approached me, and we began working together to right this terrible wrong. American Humane made unrelenting inquiries and then reached out to the local community where the adoption had occurred. We made a public announcement, making the family who'd adopted Matty a generous offer to return Matty to Brent, then waited weeks and weeks, but no one called. We refused to give up. Thanks to our continued efforts—and crusading national media coverage by the *New York Post*'s Maureen Callahan, VFW Radio, and Fox's Greta Van Susteren—the family returned Matty to Brent.

Seeing the powerful effects of this reunion redoubled my resolve to change the law once and for all so that the brave warriors who served together on the battlefield protecting our freedom could continue their journey together on the home front, enjoying the healthy, happy retirement they so richly earned.

American Humane and members of Congress, including Rep. Gus Bilirakis, Rep. Henry Cuellar, Rep. Frank LoBiondo, and Sen. Claire McCaskill, successfully worked together to amend the National Defense Authorization Act to mandate that our heroic military working dogs be returned to US soil upon retirement and that their human handlers and their families—who these dogs mean more to than anyone else—are given first right of adoption. The law was signed into law by President Obama in late 2015.

The National Defense Authorization Act was not just a political victory but a deeply human (and humane) one as well. Read what Brent's mother wrote to me about Brent and Matty after they had been reunited in the period when we were working to convince Congress to change the law and you will see for yourself how important and life changing this effort was:

**Dear Dr. Ganzert,**

**My son, Brent Grommet, left for Afghanistan in November 2013. He had a partner, a four-legged battle**

buddy named Matty. As you know, my son's partner—
the one that trained with him, shared his bed, protected
him, and made Brent stop breathing when he had
to send Matty into a culvert to check for IEDs—was
wrongfully given to someone else. My son's world col-
lapsed. He stopped talking to friends and family, he lost
his smile, and his heart was shattered. There was little
conversation. My husband searched for 13 months
trying to find someone to listen, someone to help. My
husband found you and American Humane.

Robin, you listened, you helped, and Matty was
returned to Brent on 11-14-2014, at 11:30 PM. The
next day, when we sat with you at Cracker Barrel for
breakfast, you were the first stranger Brent spoke to
since his return from Afghanistan. I sat next to my son
that day; he was talking to you, and I saw something I
hadn't seen in a long, long time. I saw my son returning.

Matty has helped my son in a way only soldiers
know how to do. I can't explain it, only to say this:
Together they trained, together they protected each
other, and together they went to hell and back. One
of them was staying awake while the other slept. They
watched each other's backs, alerting each other to
immediate life-threatening danger. As soldiers, they
did what soldiers do: They fought battles, cleared roads,
lost 17 friends, and were injured together. They won't
speak of their deployment, only to each other. But late
at night, when Brent finds himself back in war, it takes
a nudge from a wet nose to say I'm here. It's okay. And
when Matty's legs twitch, and he whimpers, and then
the whimpers turn into growls and snaps, it takes a soft
word from Brent: Matty, it's okay. Then Matty snuggles
closer to touch Brent, and both drift back to sleep.

*continued*

When they arrived home from Afghanistan, Brent remembered every painful detail. Due to standard military procedure, they were to be given 10 minutes to say goodbye. At that point in time, Matty didn't know what was going on. Brent did, however; he felt as though a huge part of him had been ripped apart. Matty was placed in an all-metal cage. As soon as the door closed, Brent heard something he had never heard before, Matty was screaming, frantically trying to dig his way out of the metal cage. Then Matty started to bite at the door. Brent continued to hear the screams for another 30 seconds as the truck drove away. My son has told me he has only cried three times in his military career. This was one of the times.

On a separate occasion, Brent was doing laundry when the door to his bedroom closed behind him. Matty was in the bedroom. In the time it takes to load a washer and start it, Matty had crushed the doorknob with his teeth and splintered the doorframe. Again, it was to find Brent and be by his side. These two together do more for each other than any doctor, therapist, or counselor could ever do in a lifetime. In four months, Brent met with you in Palm Beach, Florida. I never thought Brent would travel again.

This bond was born in the United States Army, welded in war, sealed in the blood of Afghanistan. This bond will never be broken. Being separated for 15 months didn't damage it. These two soldiers NEED to be together.

Please tell Washington that our military men and women NEED their partner dogs.

If they don't listen, try again. Keep trying until someone, like yourself, hears you. It might take months—years—but in the end, you will save lives, as you did with Brent and Matty. Soldiers need soldiers to help heal.

Thank you for saving my son, SPC Brent Grommet, and my grandson, SGT Matty, US Army.

Forever grateful,
Debbie Grommet

Over the years, American Humane helped reunite dozens of retired war dogs and their brave handlers, but for me, Matty and Brent will always hold a special place in my heart and in our 100-plus years of work to help and support our country's human and animal warriors. It's another example of how a historic mission can be updated to stay relevant and impactful. If you'd like to help increase that impact and learn more about the needs that still exist for our two-legged and four-legged veterans, including our Pups4Patriots program to save dogs in need of forever homes by training them as service animals for retired warriors struggling with PTS and traumatic brain injury, please visit www.AmericanHumane.org/military.

## MILITARY DOG RETIREMENT:
### Hundreds of Dogs Serve in War and Deserve to Retire with the Soldiers Who Cared for Them.

One hundred years ago, the guns fell silent in Europe. The Great War was over. Twenty million men lay dead, with twice that many wounded. Four of the world's great empires were gone. The toll of the war allowed communism to gain a foothold in Russia. Its aftermath led to the rise of Nazism in Germany. The Spanish flu epidemic, spread by the conditions of the war and returning soldiers, killed at least 50 million more.

In addition to the unprecedented human cost of the war, animals—specifically horses—suffered like never before. Cavalry was a major part of war for centuries, yet the invention and widespread use of the machine gun by the start of World War I made men on horseback easy targets. Approximately 8 million horses were killed as a result.

It was against this backdrop of widespread equine slaughter that then-US Secretary of War Newton D. Baker requested that American Humane, the country's first humane organization, go to Europe to help treat and save wounded horses. Through basic veterinary practices and care, its volunteers were able to save the lives of countless horses and—when necessary—to spare others from long and agonizing suffering from their wounds.

While the animals used in war have changed over the past century, the need to support them has not. Today, canines are the most important animal in war. In contrast to horses, which were easy targets for the enemy's weapon of choice, dogs are the perfect animal to help defend US troops from the enemy's most potent weapon today: the improvised explosive device. These hidden bombs are the "number-one threat," said retired Adm. Mike Mullen, former chairman of the Joint Chiefs of Staff. IEDs have been responsible for roughly two-thirds of US military casualties in Iraq and Afghanistan.

Dogs' sense of smell is roughly 50 times better than that of humans, meaning they can sniff out IEDs before the bombs have an opportunity to do any damage. Acting alone, the military only locates about half of the IEDs planted in Afghanistan and Iraq. But with dogs, the detection rate increases to 80 percent. They are an invaluable asset for freedom of movement of our ground patrols, says the Department of Defense.

Understandably, these military working dogs and their handlers develop a strong kinship on the battlefield. Inexplicably, reuniting them after their respective tours of duty is difficult.

Despite promises from the military that they would be reunited after their respective discharge, military working dogs have been adopted out without giving first choice to their former handlers. According to a Department of Defense inspector general report released in the spring, of the 232 military working dogs who served in the tactical explosive device detection program from 2011 to 2014, only 40 were adopted by handlers. Nearly 50 were adopted out to civilians, 70 went to other Army units, at least nine died, and the rest went to law enforcement agencies. The IG faulted the Army for not having plans in place to discharge the dogs.

A *New York Post* investigation in 2016 found that at least 200 handlers lost their dogs when they were secretly adopted out to civilians by military contractors. As a result, hundreds

*continued*

of handlers have searched in vain for their dogs. These include Army veteran Andrew Spaulding, who tried and failed to reunite with his bomb detection dog, Bono, with whom he served in Afghanistan. Army veteran Ryan Henderson even offered $5,000 cash plus a new German shepherd to the North Carolina family who adopted his military working dog, Satan, to no avail.

Even after American Humane prompted Congress in the 2016 National Defense Authorization Act to require that military working dogs be offered to their former handlers first, financial and logistical hurdles often remain.

While military working dogs aren't killed in action at the scale of their animal predecessors a century ago, they play just as important a role today by supporting our troops both on the battlefield and in the personal battles that can follow. They should be reunited after they are discharged, so they can enjoy retirement together.[13]

---

13  https://www.washingtonpost.com/outlook/2018/11/12/hundreds-dogs-serve-war-they-deserve
-retire-with-soldiers-who-cared-them/?utm_term=.ecce1d0f38b0

# Hiring Exceptional Talent

"The secret of my success is that we've gone to exceptional lengths to hire the best people in the world."

—Steve Jobs

Good leadership is a crucial component to success in every organization. Inspired leaders drive change by setting bold goals and forming a dynamic culture that inspires teams to surpass expectations.

In the precarious financial situation that American Humane was in, I knew I needed a group of leaders that could help our organization bounce back. A case study in this kind of leadership comes from an instantly recognizable name: Steve Jobs. Although we recall Steve at the pinnacle of his success—bespectacled and wearing a black turtleneck, blue jeans, and New Balance sneakers, introducing Apple's latest tech gadget on stage—he too suffered through treacherous lows. Steve's ingenuity, grit, and determination are what helped him overcome his own failure, and they're what I needed in my leadership team.

When the innovative Apple Macintosh computer failed in the marketplace, Steve was removed from his position leading the Macintosh team, and shortly after—in 1985—he left Apple. But, as it turned out, the fire to innovate still burned deep within him. In 2005, he told Stanford's graduating class, "I even thought about running away from [Silicon] Valley. But something slowly began to dawn on me. I still loved what I did. The turn of events at Apple had not changed that one bit. And so I decided to start over."

Starting over for Steve meant founding a new computer company, NeXT, which would push the boundaries of both hardware and software.[14] It also meant acquiring the Graphics Group from Lucasfilm and turning it into the wildly successful Pixar Animation Studios. The team at Pixar dreamed of creating a fully computer-animated film, but no one was making the technology that could do it. So Steve pushed Pixar to develop innovative new hardware, like the Pixar Image Computer, that could create computer-animated films. Then, Steve negotiated a three-movie deal with Disney. When production on their first big project, *Toy Story*, stalled, Steve Jobs personally funded the project until Disney rejoined the endeavor. When *Toy Story* finally debuted in 1995—as the first ever feature-length film to be entirely computer animated—it grossed over $370 million worldwide. Pixar became a cinematic powerhouse known around the world for its endearing stories and cutting-edge graphics.

When Steve Jobs left Apple, he didn't try to run the same playbook that led to failure. He rewrote the script for an entirely different industry, bringing his technical expertise and business savvy to Hollywood. While Steve trailblazed, Apple declined. In 1989, it experienced its first ever drop in sales, which caused the company's stock price to plummet 20 percent. The company struggled as it introduced a variety of underperforming products and went through several changes in CEOs.

Just weeks away from bankruptcy in 1997, Apple purchased NeXT—in part to entice Steve Jobs back to the company he had cofounded, first as an advisor, then as interim CEO. While serving as interim CEO, Jobs restructured the company's product lines and began a winning streak that brought Apple back to profitability, rolling out the iMac, the iPod, the iPhone, iTunes, and more.

In 1997, Apple was on the brink of shutting its doors and calling it quits. Two decades later, in 2018, that same company had annual revenues of $265.6 billion, and there were a whopping 1.3 billion active

---

14   https://simson.net/ref/NeXT/aboutnext.htm

Apple devices. The impact of Steve's leadership is still felt there and around the world.

At American Humane, I wanted a team of leaders with Steve Jobs's energy, foresight, and work ethic. I also wanted to borrow a page from his game plan. In addition to being a visionary and a great leader, Steve knew he had to hire phenomenal people at all levels of the organization. He left behind a dedicated team of employees at all levels who have kept the company thriving to this day.

Guy Kawasaki, who worked on the Macintosh team in the 1980s, learned a lot from Steve, including that "A players hire A+ players." According to Kawasaki, "A players hire people even better than themselves. It's clear, though, that B players hire C players so they can feel superior to them, and C players hire D players. If you start hiring B players, expect what Steve called 'the bozo explosion' to happen in your organization." In other words, hiring bad leaders can perpetuate a bad work ethic and an uninspired vision and, ultimately, can end an organization.[15]

Beyond Guy and Steve's anecdotal experience, there's evidence that hiring B players can hurt organizations more than you may think. A study of 190 managers found that those who feel they are unqualified for their job delegate tasks to subordinates that they also deem unqualified.[16] Incompetence can compound in an organization. It's of paramount importance, then, not only to hire those who are qualified but to make sure they are empowering effective employees.

At American Humane, I wanted to hire leaders to help me steer the organization; I couldn't do it by myself. Too many CEOs try to move the world by themselves instead of delegating important tasks to the fantastic people they hire. In a survey of 332 companies, roughly half were concerned with their employees' ability to delegate.[17] Many managers worry that the work won't be quite right unless they do it themselves.

---

15  https://guykawasaki.com/what-i-learned-from-steve-jobs/
16  https://www.sciencedirect.com/science/article/pii/S0191886915004432
17  https://www.i4cp.com/news/2007/06/26/you-want-it-when

That's not a worry without merit. Managers in the United States spend, on average, 14 percent of their time correcting mistakes made by their subordinates, according to a survey from SHL, a psychometric testing company.[18]

But delegating—and delegating to the right people—is an essential part of any company. It's not just about handing off tasks but about giving responsibility to qualified leaders to boost productivity and output. A Jordanian study of 160 municipal employees found that those who received delegated authority were more efficient, effective, and empowered.[19] Additionally, by delegating decision-making authority to more employees, organizations can increase their own stability, especially in the event that a top manager goes on leave or is out of pocket.

Many nonprofits fail to delegate effectively. And, even worse, they consolidate decision-making authority in the boards, becoming overly reliant on them to steer their organizations. They shouldn't. Leadership teams at nonprofits should be at the helm, navigating through uncertainty and plotting out a path to success.

That doesn't mean that nonprofit boards are unimportant—far from it—just that they perform a different role from your C-suite team. The members of the governing board are there to provide the fiduciary duties of care, loyalty, and obedience. According to the Association of Governing Boards, this translates into making "careful, good-faith decisions in the best interest of the institution consistent with its public or charitable mission, independent of undue influence from any party or from financial interests."[20]

In practice, the board approves the organization's strategic direction but does not develop it. It's up to the leadership team to develop an organization's strategic direction and present it to the board. It's the leadership

---

18   https://www.ncbi.nlm.nih.gov/pmc/articles/PMC5461250/

19   https://www.researchgate.net/profile/Akif_Khasawneh/publication/282466762_The_impact_of _the_delegation_of_authority_on_employees'_performance_at_great_Irbid_municipality_case _study/links/5803c02f08ae1c5148d09b16.pdf

20   https://www.agb.org/briefs/fiduciary-duties

team that should provide all the inspiration for social good, social change, and social impact. They're the men and women hired by the board to be the experts, to know how to achieve a mission in the social good space. The board hires the CEO to bring the mission to light. Institutions can falter when they don't have an inspired CEO, who's on fire for the mission, or when they have a board that tries to run the organization instead of empowering the staff and the leadership to do so.

To my great fortune—and to the great fortune of American Humane—I recruited John Payne to be my new board chair. John was president and CEO of Banfield Pet Hospital, and he had previously been president and general manager of Bayer Healthcare's Animal Health Division for North America. He was a recognized and highly respected leader in the animal care industry.

And he's still my board chair today. As board chair, John said it straight: "We've got to run this like we would a business." He gave me the latitude I needed to continue to execute on the bold initiatives of the transformational agenda we had embarked on. This included remaking staff, leadership, programs, financial structures—everything. All our operations from head to toe had to be made over. John gave me the freedom to do that and to make good decisions.

Soon after I settled into my role as CEO for American Humane, I started to build and reorganize my own leadership team. For the most part, the existing team wasn't composed of leaders by training or by trade. This is in great part why we had to engage in the exercise of remaking our mission and programs to survive. We got our leadership team on the same page when we reached agreement on embracing the idea of principled leadership. The commitment we had to principled management within the leadership team is an overarching principle that can be applied to tremendous effect in any kind of organization, whether nonprofit or for-profit; it doesn't matter the tax status.

I hired a new general counsel, a corporate relations officer, a chief communications officer, a director of marketing and e-philanthropy, and senior philanthropic advisors. I knew we needed to have a chief financial officer based in our headquarters, so I started recruiting for that. I promoted the existing human resources director to be my new chief of staff. I specifically wanted her for the position because our human capital—our people—would be critical to the success of our entire transformation endeavor.

On the program side, I created a new organizational structure designed to provide leadership for the four program planks. I experienced a stroke of particularly good fortune when a former leader at American Humane during the 1990s—and a visionary in animal welfare and veterinary medicine—approached me. She had recently retired from her position as president and CEO of a major animal philanthropy. She said to me, "You know, I love this institution so much. It's so important. I want to come on and serve the cause." So she became my chief veterinary advisor.

By February 2012, I had all of these hires in place with more to come. By hiring virtuous, hardworking leaders who were empowered to fulfill their roles, we ensured success in implementing our mission, nurturing a positive culture, reorganizing our programs, getting our finances in order, and building our brand.

## LEADERSHIP VALUES—A TIPPING POINT

Before we could bring about wholesale change across the organization, it was essential that the American Humane leadership team set an example of principled values that everyone would be expected to follow. To that end, in early January 2011—before my first board meeting—I held a facilitated planning retreat to discuss institutional goals and shared values for the leadership team.

As a leadership team, we agreed to set the example of principled leadership with clearly defined parameters for ourselves, our staff, our volunteers, our partners, our donors, and others in the American Humane community. The following leadership values helped guide our decision making in the difficult years to come:

- We embrace the diversity of our community, our ideas, and our backgrounds.

- We share a pride in the historical legacy and a passion for stewardship of our mission and reputation capital.

- Achieving sustainability, financial viability, and relevance is our course of action while innovation drives our direction.

- We act with integrity and pursue excellence in all we do.

- Together, we embark on a passionate crusade.

Going through such a significant transformation, I felt we needed to have rules of the road across all forms of leadership at American Humane—for the governing board, the executive leadership team, and the managers and supervisors out in the field. We wanted to clearly say up front that, as we transformed our organization, we embraced diversity—diversity of our community, our ideas, and our backgrounds—as we made hard decisions and developed institutional goals.

We created a new manifesto—"Transforming Our World Through Compassion"—reframing the entire institution. We asked our people to deliver on this new declaration of our core beliefs, which demanded new behavior to help ensure that change happened. In just one example, an idea that our culture had not at all wrapped itself around in any meaningful sense was the word *accountability*. People weren't accountable for achieving the goals of the organization, much less their own work goals. This would have to change. We encouraged our leaders to put a new emphasis on rebuilding our culture around the following six organizational core values:

- Compassion: Be kind and caring in our interactions with others.

- Accountability: Hold ourselves to the highest standards. Follow through on commitments and own our actions, behavior, and decisions.

- Respect for all: Be professional, listen to others, and honor diversity in all its forms.

- Loyalty to our mission: Stay focused on our purpose and our mission; our nation's most vulnerable depend on us.

- Honesty, integrity, and trust: Demonstrate transparency as trusted stewards of donor resources, supporting our leadership and one another.

- Sustainability: Make American Humane a great place to work while achieving our shared mission and goals to make a difference, now and in the future.

We would also honor our historical legacy and work to preserve and enhance it. We would do this by making really strong, smart, and sophisticated decisions as part of this roadmap that recognized and paid tribute to those visionary individuals who founded the institution and who also fought hard battles along the way. They put themselves on the line to protect children and animals in the most unimaginable circumstances.

A very important part of our principled leadership values was recognizing that we had to achieve sustainability—not just for the short term. Sustainability had to become part of our leadership manifesto for the long term. Prior leadership had not achieved sustainability, despite philanthropist H. Guy Di Stefano's gift of more than $35 million to the organization in 2006. Instead of ensuring that this gift would be used wisely to help maintain American Humane for generations to come, they spent it—and quickly. It was paramount for me to be sure that survivability, sustainability, and relevance were going to be absolutely considered in the future decisions we were going to make together as a leadership team.

We also talked about principled leadership as defining the programmatic work to be absolutely aligned to the mission and as being accountable to constituents. These principle leadership statements were so critical that they would routinely come up in each of our hard conversations about cutting programs and help guide our decision making.

We agreed to act with integrity and pursue excellence going forward, and we framed our organizational transformation in the very powerful narrative of a compassion crusade. We had to get our institution buttoned up, because we were leaders in a compassion crusade, and we had constituents who were counting on us far more than were our financial stakeholders. Our constituents were the voiceless, and if we didn't get our act together, there would be no one to give them a voice.

Our principled leadership values were a wakeup call for American Humane. I decided to put them out first and foremost, recognizing that the turnaround ahead of us was going to be, on some days, very bloody and, on some days, very painful. It would definitely not be a walk in the park for any of us. We had to agree on a working manifesto of leadership, and these principled leadership values would be our guiding force—our light to shine on the long path laid out before us.

## KEY TAKEAWAYS

- Hire and empower qualified, hardworking leaders who can see programs through.
- Delegate authority and decision-making abilities throughout an organization to boost productivity and shore up structural integrity.
- Don't let your board and your C-suite do the same work. Ensure that your board is fulfilling its fiduciary duties and that your leaders are managing the day-to-day operations.

## VOICES FOR AMERICAN HUMANE
### TOM KEARNEY

United States Navy Rear Admiral Thomas Kearney (Ret.) is a decorated veteran with more than 30 years of service in the Armed Forces, who brings a wealth of experience and expertise to the American Humane Board of Directors. His extensive firsthand military knowledge informs

American Humane's Lois Pope LIFE Center for Military Affairs, which administers a wide array of programs and initiatives assisting America's service men and women, veterans, and military animals.

Tom is the president and founder of Kearney Group, LLC, a successful independent consulting company advising and supporting over a dozen large and small defense-related businesses. During his time in the US Navy, he spent 22 years in the operational Submarine Force and 12 years directing acquisition programs at the Naval Sea Systems Command.

We asked Tom to share his experience with American Humane and his insights on effective leadership.

> American Humane is the nation's premier animal welfare organization, and it is powered through hard work and effective leadership. Ten years ago, American Humane was losing money, operating in the red, and collapsing financially despite a tremendous heritage of supporting animal welfare programs for more than 120 years. A new team came into the organization and thanks to their dynamic leadership, American Humane is now a top-rated charity with 91 cents of every dollar spent going directly into programs that help animals.
>
> As a member of American Humane's Board of Directors, I am honored to be a part of this great non-profit and have seen firsthand how this organization's superb leadership carries out their responsibilities. Leadership is a broad topic with enough books written about it to fill numerous libraries. As a former Navy Submarine Commander and Rear Admiral, I offer my thoughts on leadership and how it fits into the programmatic success at American Humane.
>
> I learned leadership operating and commanding a US nuclear submarine. The hurdles associated with some of the most technically challenging operations

possible—including intelligence, reconnaissance, arctic operations, anti-submarine warfare, and extremely shallow water operations—all taught me about effective leadership. However, the core tenets of leadership transcend any specific field or endeavor. The level of success achieved by any leader begins with the recognition of their specific responsibilities in two foundational areas: Outward Leadership and Inward Leadership, or how you lead others and how you lead yourself.

**Outward Leadership** involves two fundamental responsibilities:

1.  Establishing the culture of your organization, which drives both how people treat each other and those outside your organization; and

2.  Removing obstacles in the way of your team getting their job done.

*Everything* can be put into these two bins. Ensure that within your organization there is a healthy level of respect, drive, and a commitment to excellence. When facing the public, make sure your culture doesn't undercut your mission. As a leader, remove obstacles such as inadequate training, improper tools and equipment, onerous HR processes, substandard personnel support, toxic internal culture, and overly demanding technical processes. All can prevent your employees from fulfilling their jobs and representing your organization appropriately.

For **Inward Leadership** the most important factor is professional competence. Whether you are in business, manufacturing, engineering, medicine, military, food service, or transportation, you need to be professionally competent as a leader. You owe it to your team to know your job in detail and with a high degree of competence. Leaders have a responsibility to make the best decisions possible for their organization. So while you do not need to know it all, you do need to know when to learn more and bring yourself up to speed. There is a refrain commonly quoted in the Navy that illustrates this well: *On each ship, there is one person, who in the time of emergency, or peril on the sea, can turn to no other. He (She) is the Commanding Officer. Earning the highest, time honored seafaring title—CAPTAIN.*

Commanding officers of US Navy warships are trained to be the best captains they can be. They are personally responsible for knowing as much as possible about the complex operations of their ships. And they need to master the human side of leadership as well, effectively managing their crew through additional reading, researching, talking to other COs, and personal development. Commanding officers must prepare so that when challenging times come, they make the right decisions.

If the Outward and Inward Leadership skills are in place, then, and only then, can a leader build on all the other aspects of a successful organization like vision, team building, and developing and executing the best strategy.

Robin has filled American Humane's management level positions with officers and directors fully aligned with these two basic leadership principles, which has placed American Humane on a solid path to continued success.

# Cultivating a Positive Environment

"The goal is not simply for you to cross the finish line but to see how many people you can inspire to run with you."

—Simon Sinek

I am a big fan of town hall meetings, especially when new executives and programs need to be introduced. Employees can get to know the new people or programs in greater depth, and they have a unique opportunity to ask questions and engage with leadership. I called my first town hall as soon as the interim CEO officially departed.

I brought along my brand-new chief communications officer, who was just a week into his job. To help sweeten the introductory meeting, I brought everyone attending the town hall individual tins of my favorite handmade Moravian cookies; it was my way of letting them know I was looking forward to starting a new chapter together with them. About 175 people attended, and I was excited to meet with my new team.

When I walked into the meeting, however, I couldn't help but notice that many of the attendees had their arms crossed and weren't smiling. Some stared at the floor and avoided making eye contact with me. They looked defeated and discouraged. I immediately knew I would have my work cut out for me in terms of culture. The changes we would need to make to ensure the long-term viability of American Humane would disrupt the status quo fundamentally and forever. Those employees who were deeply invested in the way things were might not be of a mind to change it, regardless of the fact that the status quo would kill our organization sooner than anyone in the room could ever imagine.

I started the meeting by giving an inspirational opening talk about the great past and bright future of American Humane. I explained some of the plans that we had already formulated for extending our mission in some areas—while cutting back in others—which would allow us to attract a larger donor base. Then I opened up the floor to questions.

Much to my surprise, instead of a warm welcome, I was greeted with much skepticism and resistance. In retrospect, I should have expected employees who were so invested in the status quo to be extremely wary of change—and of the messenger (me), who was proposing that we embrace it. I didn't realize at the time, however, just how invested they were in the old ways of doing things.

When I opened the floor to questions, they flew fast and furious from the employees in attendance. But, instead of hope for the future, I heard a staff that felt defiant. Instead of excitement about the changes that would ensure our organization's existence for another 100 years, I heard reluctance and even resistance. Instead of a clear direction forward, I heard employees who had been without real leadership for far too long.

It was clear to me that the employees at our Denver headquarters were pessimistic about the future. I imagine they had been told many times that things would get better, but the situation had been getting worse for some time. I knew that we couldn't put American Humane on the path to success without employees who were positive, motivated, and willing to change.

## CULTURAL EROSION

I wanted to hear directly from the employees—to get their thoughts, feelings, and perspectives on the organization's present, past, and future. We needed fresh ideas and a new commitment to working together to dig out of a very deep hole; the old culture was broken and needed to be fixed. Its effect on employee morale, engagement, and performance was tremendously damaging.

Comments posted by the employees on a popular company-rating website regarding the state of American Humane before I arrived on the scene are telling:

> "There is very little communication between the various departments and between various members of senior management and lower-level staff. This makes it extremely difficult to be as effective as possible."

> "Total mismanagement of funds and the organization as a whole. Huge financial losses over the past 3 years have put the organization in peril. A 35-million-dollar bequest was squandered in less than 3 years."

> "Weak board."

> "[The organization] was nearly on the verge of closing its doors this past year due to mismanagement of a bequest [that] allowed the organization to grow beyond its means in the 5 years leading up to the new CEO's leadership."

> "Under the [previous] regime, senior management was constantly worried about taking a position on any issue, people were hired that did not know what they were doing, and [it was], in general, a very unhappy place to work. Everyone seemed to be looking down at each other. It was constant politics inside the office."

I had been caught off guard by the discouraging reception I received at the Denver town hall meeting and by the disenchantment that had been created by a lack of leadership and communication. I felt that by telling the truth about the organization and by being as transparent as

I could possibly be—describing in detail the dire financial situation we were in, the mistakes that had been made in the past, the money that had been squandered, and the changes that would need to be made to save American Humane—I would be able to open these discouraged hearts and minds.

The depth of the disengagement became apparent when the first major disaster requiring our help under my leadership struck. On March 11, 2011, a magnitude 9.0 earthquake occurred off the coast of Japan. This earthquake led to a 49-foot-high tsunami that overwhelmed and devastated the coast of Honshu, the largest of Japan's islands. More than 15,000 people died, hundreds of thousands of people were displaced from their homes, and the nation sustained hundreds of billions of dollars in damage. If that wasn't enough, the natural disaster resulted in a meltdown of the Fukushima Daiichi nuclear power plant and the deadly release of radiation into the ground and atmosphere.

The human toll was terrible and tragic. Pets and other animals were also dramatically affected by the earthquake, tsunami, and radiation. Many animals perished in the disaster, and many other animals wandered the countryside aimlessly or were relinquished to shelters overwhelmed by the magnitude of the tragedy. Immediately following the disaster, we sent a huge shipment of supplies and donations to relief agencies in Japan that had taken on the urgent task of saving the lives of animals in jeopardy. When I first reached out to our external media counsel, however, to figure out a strategy for helping the people in Japan who were helping the animals, I was told that I should call back on Monday; they didn't work on weekends.

Our new chief communications officer had a similar experience with his team. Soon after I hired him to take over our communications operations, he met with his staff to put together an emergency contact list with everyone's home or cell phone numbers. Now that we're in the age of the 24-hour news cycle, he explained, opportunities or crises can occur any day of the week, morning or night, Saturdays or Sundays. He told the team that he would treat them respectfully but that he wanted to have their personal phone numbers on file in the event the organization (and the animals we help) needed them when a crisis hit. The answer he got in response from one employee was, "You don't pay me enough to have my home phone number."

Coming from an always-on-call background at international news organizations and major nonprofits, our chief communications officer was stunned, not just that someone would actually say that to a new boss but more that they would care so little about the lifesaving work they had been hired to support.

As a national nonprofit that is dedicated to saving the lives of animals, we routinely deal with crises. There's always a crisis of some sort somewhere in our great nation or around the globe where we're called to action. We need to move quickly when there are animals in crisis; a delay of hours or even minutes can mean lost lives. But if our team was going to resist that—refusing to be available on weekends or to provide us with a way to reach them whenever a crisis hit—then that, to me, was an unacceptable situation.

Ultimately, we had to rebuild not only that department but other departments that didn't feel the sense of urgency I certainly felt to execute on our mission of saving the lives of animals. Making these changes enabled us to begin to turn the tide of the toxic culture that deeply infused American Humane.

Washington, D.C., is full of trade associations and nonprofit organizations that do a lot. They stay very busy, but too many don't accomplish as much as they could. Yes, everybody's busy; they just don't all make a significant or measurable difference. Billions of dollars in this town get wasted due to bureaucracies, ineptitude, and a lack of accountability. I would not allow American Humane to become one of those organizations. Whether you're a secretary or the CEO, each of us owns our results.

## EMOTIONALLY EXHAUSTED

A study published in *The Journal of Applied Behavioral Science* measured the psychological capital—the hope, efficacy, optimism, and resilience—of 132 employees from numerous businesses and organizations. They found that employees who had high levels of psychological capital were more likely to be emotionally engaged and less likely to be cynical about their work. Additionally, those same employees were more likely to engage in organizational citizenship behaviors, like welcoming new employees, and less likely to engage in workplace deviance behaviors, like keeping work-related information from coworkers or intentionally squandering an organization's resources.[21] The negativity in that town hall led me to believe that many employees were low on psychological capital.

I didn't let myself get bogged down by the resistance that I encountered early on. I realized that some Denver employees who attended the town hall would need to improve their attitudes and build up their psychological capital, or they would not be with me very long. From the leadership team down through the lower-level staff, this was not the group that I would be excited about going to work with every day. The dysfunctional culture that had sucked the inspiration right out of our people left them disheartened and without direction. Would they be effective change agents in the social space? I knew that I needed to cultivate a positive culture, one that nourished my employees and built up their reservoirs of psychological capital.

In his book *The 7 Habits of Highly Effective People*, Stephen Covey writes about the idea of the emotional bank account. Just as we make periodic deposits into and withdrawals from our *financial* bank account, we do the same with our *emotional* bank account. According to Covey, an emotional bank account is "a metaphor that describes the amount of trust that's been built up in a relationship. It's the feeling of safeness you have with another human being."

I personally believe that Covey really hit the nail on the head. People

---

21   https://digitalcommons.unl.edu/cgi/viewcontent.cgi?article=1031&context=managementfacpub

naturally, every day and in every walk of life, deal with emotional bank accounts whether they know it or not. When you encounter a stranger on the street, you've got a zero balance in your emotional bank account with that person; it's neither positive nor negative. But, if you walk down the street, and you nod your head or smile at the stranger and he smiles back, then you've both made tiny deposits in your emotional bank accounts.

All of us have established emotional bank accounts with our coworkers, our boss, our friends, our family, and our loved ones—everyone we interact with. And these emotional bank accounts can have either a positive or negative balance. Very rarely if ever would they have a zero balance.

According to Covey, examples of deposits that we might make into someone's emotional bank account include the following:

- Displaying kindness and courtesy
- Keeping promises
- Clear expectations
- Loyalty to the absent
- Apologizing

And examples of withdrawals include these:

- Displaying unkindness and discourtesy
- Breaking promises
- Unclear expectations
- Showing disloyalty or duplicity
- Exhibiting pride, conceit, or arrogance

Consider the example of a spouse or significant other. We make deposits all day long when we're listening and paying attention to them. And we're making deposits when we give them a gift or make them dinner or just sit on the couch and watch TV with our arm around them. That's making deposits.

In the same way, we make withdrawals with people all the time. When we're late for a meeting, we make a withdrawal from the emotional bank account. When we promised to do something and then didn't do it, we make another withdrawal. Balances are going up and down all the time, but most of the time, those balances stay positive, because we all try to do the best we can for our coworkers, friends, and loved ones.

Unfortunately, there are times when the bank account goes negative, causing a big problem for a leader. When your financial bank account goes negative, you're overdrawn, and you need to make a deposit immediately, so your checks don't bounce. It's the same for your emotional bank account. When you overdraw it, you need to do something to correct it immediately and get it back into the positive. That's when you send your spouse flowers or a thoughtful gift, or when you stay after work late to make up for a project that you didn't complete on time.

Despite our best efforts, there will always be times when things get so bad between people that their emotional bank accounts go bankrupt. That's when you've made so many withdrawals on an account that making deposits won't bring that balance back to positive again. This is a situation that every leader must avoid at all costs. When things get this bad, then the leader has failed in some way, and they must take a close look at what that failure was (a bad hire, insufficient training, inadequately addressing a stakeholder's concerns?) and then make sure lessons are learned so that it doesn't happen again.

According to Covey, there are two keys to making deposits:

- Key 1: Deposits need to be frequent and consistent.
- Key 2: Deposits do not occur until the recipient considers it a deposit.

When you reward and recognize your people for doing a good job, be sure to keep the idea of emotional bank accounts in mind. Are you making deposits into your people's accounts, or are you making withdrawals? And what about the managers and supervisors who work for you? Are they making deposits or withdrawals with the people who work for them?

Robin touring Bucher Farms, an American
Humane Certified™ farm, with John Bucher

Robin with an elephant while working to expand
American Humane's conservation work in South Africa

Robin with Sarah Michelle Gellar and
Shannen Doherty at the 2019 Hero Dog Awards

Robin with a camel in Abu Dhabi

Robin with Vivica A. Fox at the 2019 Hero Dog Awards

Robin the dolphin, namesake of Robin Ganzert,
who lives at Loro Parque in Spain

Dr. Lesa Staubus, a veterinarian with American Humane's
rescue team, working with a retired Military Working Dog

Amber, an American Humane first responder,
rescuing a dog in North Carolina

An American Humane animal rescuer walking through the
devastation in the Bahamas in the wake of Hurricane Dorian

The American Humane Board with Hero Dogs Piglet and Gus at the 2019 Hero Dog Awards

Robin and her dog Mr. Darcy

Robin with Military Working Dog Isky on Capitol Hill

Robin with a turtle in Bequia in the Grenadines

The answers to these questions will largely determine whether your people will enjoy where they work, whether they will be engaged in their jobs, and whether your organization will be a success.

## CULTIVATING CULTURE

A happy workplace is made up of happy people, and happy people are productive employees. You can't staff an office with cynical ne'er-do-wells and expect that organization to thrive—or even survive. But a positive, dynamic, and mission-focused environment can enrich and energize employees.

The first step in fixing a broken, dysfunctional culture is to limit the negativity that often infests the organization and to stop dwelling on the past. True recovery begins with a healthy acceptance of the situation, along with the will to move forward. Despite the fact that I had not been told about the true state of American Humane when I took over as CEO, I had accepted the situation I was in. I had a very strong will to move the organization forward, to pull us out of the deep hole that we had dug for ourselves during the years before I arrived. I needed the entire American Humane team to pull with me, for everyone to leave behind the hurt and uncertainty of the past and to move forward to a much better future. I needed everyone on deck, giving us their very best efforts.

While some people seek awesome, most people will settle for just okay. The truth is they are willing to settle for mediocrity. You can see it in their faces and hear stories of lives of quiet desperation all around us. There are plenty of books and films out there about people who stay in jobs they hate or marriages that don't work; it's a common story. In some way, they find comfort in staying in that bad spot, where the evils they know are better than the evils they don't know.

The problems happen when they bring their negative attitudes along with them into the organizations for which they work. This negativity rubs off of their lives and onto the lives of everyone around them. It can be seen in the form of dull and boring meetings, underperforming businesses, bad experiences with donors and partners in the field, and more. It makes us less effective as an organization and it dulls our impact on the world around us.

It's not that these people are intentionally forcing negativity our way; I believe that it's often an unconscious act. Unfortunately, people often don't even realize the negativity they are bringing into their own lives and into the lives of those around them. They get lost in the everyday grind of where they live, how they work, and with whom they socialize. Not everyone can break the cycle or have even decided they want to. Most don't give it much thought.

I personally believe that most people, given a choice of having a good or even great experience, would choose to have an awesome experience—both in their work life and in their personal life.

It is extremely hard work to force yourself to think positively when you are swimming against the current. It is also easy to fall prey to anger and frustration. There were many potential targets for our employees to blame as we worked to remake our culture and American Humane itself. The truth is that allowing such an attitude to continue to fester would have meant nothing but lower morale and wasted energy for our people. I needed to deal with it.

To get a different perspective, leaders must rise above the chaos and confusion that's happening on the ground. I wanted to see the forest instead of just the trees in order to help our people find their way to a better future. When you're in a maze, it's easier to find your way out if you're looking at it from above. I took the long view and avoided becoming overwhelmed by each individual problem we faced. As an example, even though I had to deal with each of American Humane's debts individually, I knew we needed to have a broader overall strategy for debt reduction.

To get a better idea of what our people were thinking—how they thought we could and should improve—we conducted a series of employee satisfaction surveys. To be perfectly honest, the results were not good at first. Many weren't pleased with the decisions I made that disrupted the status quo and remade our culture. I'm happy to say, however, that our current team has fully embraced our reason for doing what we do, and they are committed and accountable for achieving the goals we have set for ourselves as an organization.

This embrace of our purpose and our revitalized culture is reflected in the most recent employee satisfaction survey, which we conducted in 2016. The survey, which was anonymous and confidential, revealed that

- 94 percent of staff are proud of American Humane's brand.
- 92 percent of staff reported overall positive feelings toward their workplace.
- 90 percent say they are paid well.
- 100 percent of employees felt their work was meaningful.

Is there room for improvement? Of course. There always is. I wish that every one of the responses was at 100 percent. We continue to seek the input of our team to make ongoing improvements in our operations, and I hope that we'll do even better in our next employee satisfaction survey.

Another thing we did was to establish something we call Team Humane—an internal team of people who organize birthday celebrations, lunches, and team-building events for our employees. It's the idea that the group that plays together stays together. The stronger the relationships between our people—and with other stakeholders—the more loyalty and engagement we build within our team.

I regularly encourage our people to get out of their offices and to get to know one another better. If there's someone in the office they don't know very well—or even if they do know them well—take them to lunch. It doesn't have to be anything fancy or expensive; grabbing a sandwich or salad and taking it to a park is fine. While spending time with someone in their program area is good, it's also remarkably productive to cross function areas. Program people should connect with admin people and vice versa. Someone who specializes in rescues, for example, would be well served to build relationships with the folks in accounting.

When that person in rescue needs something quickly—like a check cut to get a rescue team in place—then having a relationship with someone in accounting can make all the difference in the world. It just smooths the way.

My goal is to encourage more productive, happy, healthy relationships throughout the organization. To build teamwork and reinforce our culture, we have management and professional retreats built around a central theme. For example, as the organization focused on certifying zoos, aquariums, and conservation centers around the world, we schedule management meetings at those very places and take time to tour the facility and see our mission in action. We can see for ourselves the positive impact our strategic planning and annual goalsetting have on animals when the standards for their care are elevated. When our management team is literally face to face with the animals we are charged to protect—on their own turf—it brings our mission to life in a way that's just not possible when you're sitting in a conference room.

To keep everyone connected to our mission and to reinforce our culture, we share organizational news and victories as they occur with our entire staff. If we're on the front page of *USA Today* or if I'm going to appear on the *Today Show*, that goes out to everyone on our team almost immediately. I also make a point to share news and victories with our board and key donors. It generates a sense of excitement that these are the things that we're doing, these are the victories that we're forging—step by step—and here's where we're having an impact on animals and people as we fulfill our mission.

Just as we share news in real time, we take immediate action to address problems that arise in the world related to our mission. One of many examples of this was when we received data showing that animals being shipped as air cargo were dying in disturbing numbers. We began conversations with major airlines. As a result, we are now building a certification program that will make air travel safer and more comfortable for hundreds of thousands of pets that travel every year by air.

# HIRING FOR CULTURE AND ALIGNMENT

Although I like to think that anyone has the ability to change, I do believe there's no small amount of truth in the saying "You can't teach an old dog new tricks." It's not that people who have been around the organization for a long time *can't* change; it's that they often don't see any reason *to* change. If they don't see any reason to change, they won't. Or—even worse—they'll fight change kicking and screaming all the way, actively sabotaging your efforts to transform the organization.

If you don't believe this simple truth about change, consider the statistics. According to McKinsey & Company, 70 percent of change programs fail to achieve their goals—in most cases, because of employee resistance and a lack of support from management.[22]

Given that trying to change people and align them with your new vision and mission is often a losing proposition, it's often better from the start to hire for alignment. When you hire people who are aligned with your vision and mission, your culture will be reinforced and strengthened.

How exactly can you hire the right people? The job site LinkedIn recently conducted a survey of approximately 1,300 hiring managers to determine the best behavioral interview questions to ask in six different categories: adaptability, culture add, collaboration, leadership, growth potential, and prioritization. Within the category of culture add, LinkedIn found that these five questions will help you zero in on job candidates who will bring something new to the table while aligning with your organization's existing culture:

- What are the three things that are most important to you in a job?
- Tell me about a time in the last week when you've been satisfied, energized, and productive at work. What were you doing?
- What's the most interesting thing about you that's not on your resume?

---

22  https://www.mckinsey.com/featured-insights/leadership/changing-change-management

- What would make you choose your company over others?

- What's the biggest misconception your coworkers have about you, and why do they think that?

In its report, LinkedIn warns against falling into a "hire like me" mentality when hiring for culture fit. Diversity of background and life and work experience is important. Says the LinkedIn report:

> **Instead, look for candidates who share the same beliefs and values as your organization but also bring diversity of thought and experience that will drive your company forward. We call this a "culture add." Plus, research shows that employees who are a good culture fit are more likely to stay with your company and will have greater performance and job satisfaction.**

When we hire new employees at American Humane, we look for people who are fully aligned with our purpose. People who want to work for and with us because of our mission and our values: rescuing animals that are the victims of disasters, both natural and caused by people; caring about the welfare and treatment of the animals on our farms and ranches; helping America's veterans and recognizing their heroic contributions to our country both on and off the battlefield; exploring the bond between animals and people, helping ensure the safety and humane treatment of animal actors; preserving the rich web of life essential to the survival of all the creatures of Earth; and so much more. This is the purpose that drives our culture and each and every one of us every day of the week.

## THE NATIONAL FIRE DOG MONUMENT— A CASE IN POINT

We've all grown up with the idea that firefighters and dogs—especially the Dalmatian breed—are natural work partners. There are some very good reasons for that notion. Several hundred years ago, dogs were trained to protect the occupants of the carriages of the well-to-do from thieves and bandits. They would run alongside the carriages—often for many miles—ready to protect the men, women, and children in their charge.

Initially, there was no one breed of carriage dog. Over time, however, the Dalmatians began to dominate. The Dalmatian got along particularly well with horses ("like a duck to water," according to an old AKC publication), had a good temperament, and possessed the strength and stamina required for long journeys.

When horse-drawn carriages began to be used to carry men and equipment for fighting fires, the noble Dalmatians went along with them, barking to clear people out of the way and nipping at other dogs that often tried to attack or harass the galloping horses. When horse-drawn fire carriages were eventually replaced with motorized fire engines, Dalmatians guarded the firehouse or were kept as mascots by fire departments.

Although Dalmatians are no longer a common sight in fire departments today, fire dogs do still play a vital role. They are trained to sniff out accelerants (highly flammable substances such as gasoline or turpentine) used by arsonists to commit crimes. Today, these arson dogs can be of any breed. In fact, Sadie, the 2011 American Humane Hero Dog Awards winner in the Law Enforcement/Arson category, was a black Labrador Retriever. Little did I know the role that Sadie would one day play in helping to transform the culture at American Humane.

Sadie was a nationally certified accelerant detection K-9, and she worked for the Major Crimes Unit of the Colorado Bureau of Investigation. When she was nominated for our Hero Dog Award, she had already worked approximately 400 fires, leading to numerous arrests. According to her handler, her skills were instrumental in providing critical evidence in numerous high-profile arson and homicide cases. Although Sadie didn't win the top national Hero Dog Award title in 2011, she became an inspiration to many thousands of people across the country.

Inspired by Colorado's first arson dog, Erin, Sadie's handler made it his personal mission to raise the money required to create a National Fire

Dog Monument. He sparked a movement with firefighters across our great country in support of this effort. A nonprofit was created to raise the required funds, which was wildly successful.

We were excited to lend a hand, and we completed the last tranche of funding for the National Fire Dog Monument, ensuring its completion. Says the handler, "We raised over $100,000 and are bringing recognition to these dogs, who are so important in finding out who or what is responsible for fires."[23]

After the 450-pound bronze statue—named "Ashes to Answers"— was cast, we sponsored a two-week, 12-city tour from the sculptor's home in Colorado across the United States to New York City. There, it was put on display at the New York City Fire Museum. The monument then traveled to Washington, D.C., where the statue was dedicated in 2013 and put on permanent display outside the fire station for Engine Company 2 and Rescue Squad 1, just blocks from the US Capitol building. The monument depicts a larger-than-life firefighter looking down at his trusty Labrador retriever—modeled after Hero Dog Sadie.

All of us at American Humane were, of course, very proud that Hero Dog Sadie was chosen to be a model for the National Fire Dog Monument. Our participation in the creation of the monument and its tour across the country was very exciting for our team, and it helped to build camaraderie around a common purpose.

Something occurred about a year later that had an even larger positive effect on our culture. In March 2014, the *Washington Post* held a contest to "see which one of the region's monuments stands above the rest." The contest, named Monument Madness by the *Post*, was modeled after the NCAA March Madness basketball tournament, which determines the national champion each year. A total of 32 monuments were selected for the contest, divided into four categories:

---

23    https://www.firehouse.com/home/news/10733763/from-ashes-to-answers-fire-dog-monument
-making-its-way-to-dc

- Presidents and Founding Fathers
- War and peace
- Arts and sciences
- What the heck is that?

The National Fire Dog Monument was selected by the *Post* to compete in the "What the heck is that?" category, where it was initially put up against the Women's Titanic Memorial. The challenge was real, as some of the nation's most venerated monuments—including the Washington Monument, the Lincoln Memorial, the Thomas Jefferson Memorial, the US Marine Corps War Memorial, among others—were chosen to participate in the contest. Regardless of the competition, however, we were thrilled Hero Dog Sadie's statue was included, and we were hopeful she would do well.

The National Fire Dog Monument description in the *Post* read:

> **Fighting for truth, justice, and lower insurance premiums, this detailed statue of a firefighter and his crime-solving black Lab combines a youthful vigor with the experience of working on hundreds of cases together. Don't be fooled by her cuddly appearance: This dog is always sniffing out danger and finding a way to win.**[24]

A selection committee narrowed the original group of 32 monuments down to the tournament's Sweet 16, which included the National Fire Dog Monument. Then voting opened to the public.

When the competition was first announced, our staff started following along on social media and getting inspired by Sadie's story all over

---

24  https://www.washingtonpost.com/news/going-out-guide/wp/2014/03/20/monument-madness-15
-statues-and-one-obelisk-in-a-very-washington-tournament

again. Not only had the 2011 Hero Dog Awards been a tremendously exciting TV show, showcasing the life-changing, lifesaving power of our bond with animals, but one of our dogs had inspired the development of the first-ever monument dedicated to the brave fire dogs who work across our nation. We all pulled together again in a common purpose to support Sadie and this new national tribute to bravery.

The National Fire Dog Monument was put up against Takoma Park's Roscoe the Rooster statue in the Sweet 16, and Roscoe was defeated, 960 votes to 730, taking Sadie to the Elite 8 against the flaming golden sword of the Second Division Memorial. The Elite 8 vote weighed heavily in our favor, with 680 votes going to the National Fire Dog Monument and only 237 to the Second Division Memorial.

As the *Washington Post* reported,

> **The top-seeded Second Division Memorial had good reason to fear the seventh-seed National Fire Dog Monument: After all, if there was anyone in this field capable of outmaneuvering a giant flaming sword, it was a canine who sniffs out fires for a living. Sadie knew exactly how to exploit the sword's weaknesses and did so to dominating effect.**

This put Sadie in the Final Four—up against the Jim Henson and Kermit statue on the campus of the University of Maryland, while the Lincoln Memorial and Arlington Cemetery's National Seabee Memorial squared off against each other.

The winners of this matchup? The National Seabee Memorial out-polled the Lincoln Memorial 1,390 votes to 437, and the National Fire Dog Monument dominated the Jim Henson and Kermit statue, 2,216 votes to 570, putting Sadie and the National Fire Dog Monument and the National Seabee Memorial in the finals.

As the *Washington Post* reported, more than 9,000 votes were cast to determine which monument in the Washington area was most popular.

The National Seabee Memorial leaped into an early lead, but the voting became more heated as the deadline fast approached. According to the *Washington Post*:

> Things didn't look good for Sadie early on, as the Seabees held a 600-vote lead with seven hours left in the championship round; a Seabee champagne celebration seemed like an inevitability. But votes kept pouring in for both sides, and after 13 hours, Sadie turned the deficit around to claim the title.[25]

The final tally was 5,184 votes for the National Fire Dog Monument and 4,201 votes for the National Seabee Memorial—making it the most popular monument in the nation's capital! During the course of the contest, our employees worked hard to rally votes for Hero Dog Sadie and the monument—reaching out to family and friends for support. The competition turned out to be a golden opportunity for the members of the American Humane team to personally experience the importance of our mission and what makes it so special. Additionally, it showed them how the work they do day in and day out can create something that will outlive all of us.

The excitement the *Washington Post* competition ignited within our staff was really something to see and experience. It was proof our people had fully embraced our transformative program agenda. It was also the clearest evidence yet that the organization's culture had changed to one of service to others. The focus was no longer directed inward; it had shifted outward.

Of course, it didn't hurt that being part of the creation of the National Fire Dog Monument was also a lot of fun, and the national tour of the

---

25  https://www.washingtonpost.com/news/going-out-guide/wp/2014/04/01/monument-madness -and-the-winner-is

statue was truly inspiring, generating headlines across the country. I'll never forget when the tour officially kicked off in Denver, where the monument was proudly put on display in front of the Colorado capitol building, with its golden dome. I still have a photo of two Denver Fire Department trucks, with their long ladders fully extended and a huge American flag waving down below; and there was our National Fire Dog Monument, being celebrated with hundreds of firefighters, their families, and the public. It was enough to give anyone goose bumps.

## KEY TAKEAWAYS

- An organization's culture is its foundation. Make sure it's well maintained and strong.

- Frame your purpose. Know why your organization does what it does and involve your people in creating bridges of understanding and action from that reason to the work they do every day.

- Know your organization's core values and ensure your people are fully aligned with them.

- If your culture is broken, take steps to fix it.

- Build trust with your employees using Stephen Covey's idea of the emotional bank account.

- Hire for culture and alignment.

# Building a Unique Image

"A brand for a company is like a reputation for a person. You earn reputation by trying to do hard things well."

—Jeff Bezos

There are more than 1.5 million nonprofits registered with the Internal Revenue Service, according to the National Center for Charitable Statistics, almost all competing for resources and attention.[26] As a result, the charitable sector is more crowded than ever; nonprofits must differentiate themselves.

As Jeff Bezos said, "a brand . . . is like a reputation." When I was named CEO of American Humane, I'm not sure I could have told you what our brand really was. We were trying to do too much with too little, to be too many things to our donors, staff, board, and other stakeholders. As a result, our focus was diluted and our impact reduced. We embodied a variety of different brands, depending at which particular program you were looking. Were we advocates for children's welfare? Animal rescuers? Advocates for the responsible treatment of farm animals?

Under my leadership, we shed programs where we weren't leaders because we recognized that programmatic overlap between organizations wastes resources and ultimately hurts the groups you're trying to help. In doing so, we reaffirmed our distinct position in the animal welfare space.

Branding should communicate your unique mission to the general public, to the constituencies you serve, and to donors.

## DEFINING BRAND BY THE WORK

One hundred years ago, the American Humane brand was clear and compelling. We were, among other things, the first responders for America's animals. American Humane's historic rescue program was founded in 1916 on the battlefields of World War I, when the US Secretary of War wrote to us and called us to action, enlisting us to save and care for the vitally important warhorses, mules, and donkeys who were being killed and injured in huge numbers in conflicts overseas.

We saw these animals' roles come to life in the stunning film *War Horse*, which our good friend Steven Spielberg directed and coproduced. The US Armed Forces used a surprising number of horses and mules during the war to transport supply wagons, ambulances, traveling kitchens, water carts, food, engineer equipment, light artillery, and shells. In addition to their transport duties, horses were also used in direct combat. It is estimated that some 10 million horses were killed.

In response to the Secretary of War's call, American Humane sent volunteers and considerable resources overseas to help—even before US fighting forces arrived. They were sorely needed, and the magnitude of the humanitarian crisis soon became all too apparent. Amid the carnage, our rescue workers toiled to help as many animals as they could, saving and caring for some 68,000 wounded warhorses each month. It was a pivotal and powerful moment for our organization.

Fast-forward 100 years later, and American Humane's rescue program includes a fleet of emergency response vehicles customized to help animals in disasters, specialized rescue equipment designed specifically for animal search and rescue, and a force of some 200 emergency services volunteers located across the country.

In late 2010, we had just one rescue cache, located at our former headquarters in the Denver area. The heart of that cache was Lucy, a fully self-contained 82-foot-long rescue vehicle complete with a mobile emergency veterinary hospital that can sleep 16 people. I can tell you from personal experience that she makes a huge impression when she arrives on the scene of a disaster. People have told me that when they see our big rig, they know help has arrived.

Lucy was deployed to New York City immediately after the 9/11 terrorist attacks, serving as the veterinary base for first responders and their 300 search and rescue dogs, who were desperately looking for survivors in the rubble. Each night, the search and rescue teams combing through the debris of the damaged and destroyed World Trade Center buildings would bring their animals to Lucy, where a team of veterinarians and other volunteers checked their paws for cuts and glass shards, administered first aid, and, because of all the toxic substances still burning in the pile, made sure they were thoroughly decontaminated.

Soon after arriving at American Humane, I recognized that we had a crown jewel in Lucy. I also recognized that, with time being of the essence in responding to disasters, it could often take too long for Lucy to reach disaster scenes far from Denver—on the eastern seaboard, in Southern California, or on the Gulf Coast. So, we created a new regional deployment model for rescue that put our first responders within 24 hours of any disaster—natural or otherwise—that might occur across the country. We undertook an immediate planning exercise on how to expand the American Humane Rescue program and how to continue to be the first responders anywhere in the nation.

I'm proud that we can be on the scene anywhere in the continental United States quickly; that's a significant victory for American Humane. Today, we have a total of five 50-foot regional rescue trucks able to carry rescue workers, lifesaving rescue boats, and veterinary and sheltering supplies for up to 100 animals.

On May 20, 2013, a devastating EF5 tornado touched down in Oklahoma, tearing through the city of Moore, about 10 miles south of Oklahoma City, and leaving behind a 14-mile-long path of death and destruction. Twenty-four people were killed by the storm, and 212 more were injured, not to mention an overwhelming number of animal deaths and injuries.

We brought our big rig Lucy and one of our rescue vehicles into Moore after the tornado tore through the city, setting up a giant shelter for more than 300 cats and dogs at the Oklahoma State Fairgrounds, even as more storms continued to pound the area. In between shifts, our rescue teams grabbed what sleep they could on the trucks, which also serve as sleeping quarters for our volunteers.

When Hurricane Harvey devastated Houston, Texas, in August 2017, we were first to serve. Harvey caused 106 deaths in the United States and an estimated $125 billion in damage, matching Katrina as the costliest hurricane in US history. Across the state of Texas, people abandoned their homes and communities, neighborhoods were destroyed, and dazed pets were separated from their families.

We sent a total of four teams of highly trained and experienced disaster relief workers into the fray, along with three of our animal rescue trucks. The first American Humane Rescue team worked in the Houston area, helping shelter frightened, often emaciated animals displaced by the storm. The second rushed to the City of Orange Grove, near Corpus Christi, close to ground zero, where the monster storm made landfall, working with our friends at Chicken Soup for the Soul Pet Food to deliver more than 100,000 pounds of free emergency food to shelters providing relief to animals separated from their families.

The third and fourth American Humane Rescue teams took over the operations of two mega-shelters in Louisiana housing hundreds of animals each, many of them refugees from the storm in Texas. All told, we cared for 1,000 animals left in the wake of Hurricane Harvey.

Our rigs allow us to respond to catastrophes of all kinds across the country. When not responding to disasters, the rigs become mobile health clinics, delivering free veterinary services in remote places where people cannot afford to take their four-legged family members to the vet for checkups or treatment. Our new national staging model allows us to be literally everywhere, every day for animal rescue.

We were first to serve in World War I. We were first to serve after the 9/11 tragedy. We were first to serve in Moore, Oklahoma. We were first to serve in the aftermath of Hurricane Harvey. Accordingly, in 2017, "First to Serve" officially became the new branding tagline for American Humane. By refining our programs and homing in on our unique history and distinctive work, we were able to crystallize our brand, one that appeals to donors and accurately conveys what we do.

## KEEPING OUR BRAND ALIVE

There are currently three major organizations in the country devoted to the humane treatment of animals: American Humane, the Humane Society of the United States (which spun off from American Humane in 1954), and the ASPCA (American Society for the Prevention of Cruelty to Animals). Because of the similarity of our names, American Humane was often the victim of brand confusion. People didn't necessarily understand who they were giving their donations to or that there was even a difference. My team and I are deep in the space and understand the clear distinctions between our organizations—at both the national and the local level. But the general public, for the most part, does not.

We were the country's first national humane organization and the undisputed leader in the humane field up until about two decades ago, when we lost our voice because we didn't have a clear strategic direction. When we lost our voice, we lost our brand.

This really is a tale about how leadership can make a difference in breathing life into a listless brand. Our brand is important because it represents a history, a philosophy, and an effort that led the humane movement in America not long after the Civil War.

We are also the last moderate national humane voice—one focused on science-based and commonsense humane solutions. We are the only group at the national level talking about the bond between people and animals. We are the only organization that gave working animals a voice.

The push to be first to serve is an important branding differentiator in the humane space. After 140 years, our brand needed a major refresh and renewal. There were good reasons for this action. Number one, you periodically need to reenergize and refocus the way you present your organization to the world—and to your employees. If you're changing your programs and the way you operate, you may be best served by reflecting those changes in the name, in the logo, in everything you do, and making sure that you're explaining things to people in the simplest way. While the work is complex, the branding makes it easy to love and support the mission.

Our challenge at American Humane was to stand out from other players. How could we make the organization relevant to today, when we were still using our old name, the American Humane Association? Even the word *association* in our name did little to prevent brand confusion on the part of donors—and prospective donors. We are not a trade member association in the traditional sense; we are a donor-based group.

We decided to do a deeper dive into our brand as the final icing on the cake for the transformation of American Humane. We were very fortunate, because we did have some outside help in this effort. We brought in a top-tier team, including a former marketing executive from PepsiCo, who played a critical role in the Pepsi Challenge and had major brand experience.

We applied a common branding technique called the brand wheel. This technique breaks down your brand into five categories:

- Attributes: the surface-level facts about your organization
- Benefits: the benefits that you, as a service or product provider, give to your clients and customers
- Values: the ideas that you celebrate and promote, the kind of organization you want to be
- Personality: the working style you operate with and how people solve problems together
- Brand essence: the core of who you are as an organization

We went through a formal exercise using the brand wheel. It took us much deeper into our brand than just creating a new logo. We identified the true essence of our organization.

In addition, the team conducted an in-depth analysis of our strengths and our history to reveal the available white space in our field. The white space represents the things that have not yet been claimed or that could make you unique, to differentiate your organization from the competition. We realized that our organization had some remarkable white space that none of the other institutions in the humane landscape had. In fact, the consultants told us that most organizations have to make up this white space where it doesn't really exist, because they just aren't that special. American Humane is that special.

The white space we have that no other humane organization possesses is the simple phrase "First to Serve." This tagline is obvious in some ways when you think about it. American Humane was not only the first national humane organization in the United States, but we really have been pioneers—the first—in virtually every area relating to the protection of animals. American Humane was originally founded in 1877 to work on protections for farm animals. We were the first to serve in the protection of animals in film and then television. We were the first national organization to serve in the protection of animals in the military with our work rescuing wounded warhorses overseas. We were the first to create a certification program specifically devoted to the treatment of animals in zoos and aquariums. We were first to serve the transportation industry by having a certification program for airlines to help ensure that animals are kept safe and humanely treated when they're traveling. The firsts just go on and on and on, and that unique part of our identity just surfaced as we worked to identify what white space we owned.

The tagline "First to Serve" was inspirational for the American Humane team and to stakeholders and potential donors alike. It made people realize—without lingering in the past—that we were the organization behind virtually every major advance in the humane field.

Finally, there was the matter of our name and our logo. Our branding consultants suggested that we drop the word *association* from our name, because it was no longer relevant for who or what we were. It came down to the two most powerful words in our brand essence, which are American Humane—powerful words that define an ecosystem regarding the humane movement. Out of that came our new master logo and our plan to create sub-logos for our different certification programs.

Rebranding efforts can be expensive, and with a gorgeous new tagline, "First to Serve," we had to be creative with our rebrand rollout. Unlike some organizations that raise a lot of money and spend a good deal of it on advertising and more fundraising, we put our money into programs, leaving a limited budget for advertising and marketing—essentially nothing.

We did make investments in communications, however, because one of our key charter points, and one where we focus a tremendous amount of energy, is that we're both protecting animals and working to teach the public how to protect and be good to animals in the first place. Otherwise, you're just bailing a leaky boat.

As I mentioned earlier, we condensed our 40-plus programs—which all had different themes and, in essence, brands—down to just four platform planks. This enabled us to be much more consistent in the usage of all of our branding and platforms so that we could more efficiently get the brand name into the public awareness without a major investment in advertising, marketing, and other types of paid media. Instead, we worked to generate media interest in our rescue work, expert advice, new program developments, and scientific discoveries. Using this approach, we increased the amount of news coverage by a factor of more than 700, getting us in front of millions of people through stories carried by *USA Today*, CNN, *The Washington Post*, *TIME* magazine, *Politico*, *The Hill*, *The New York Times*, and thousands of others.

There are other humane groups that spend $50 million to $100 million a year in advertising. We do not. We would much rather put funds into programs. That's why we feel our best approach when it comes to communications is to choose a route that emphasizes brains over brawn. This allows us to be more focused and smarter rather than just throwing tons of donor money at chasing more donor money. We prefer to do well with the donor dollars we have, which is just one of the reasons we have a four-star Charity Navigator rating while other national humane organizations do not.

We rolled out the new branding effort in September 2017 and immediately began to measure its impact. What we were primarily looking at were our donations. We recognized that we had an inverted pyramid. Traditional philanthropy has a donor pyramid with a few major donors at the top, a solid middle tier, and a large group of lower-level donors who make up the base. I'm pleased to report that in our first year after rolling out the new brand and logo, we moved to the traditional model by growing our low-level donors by 40 percent. We have built a very strong base of new and individual donors at that lower level of giving because of our rebranding effort.

## SPREADING THE WORD

So how did we flip that pyramid? First of all, we focused on the super brand, American Humane. One of the things our branding and marketing consultants said that was so important for me, particularly as CEO, was to push back continually on anyone who wasn't using the full phrase, "American Humane, First to Serve." Doing this ensured that First to Serve became a part of our culture.

Part of our new brand rollout was an invitation to all employees to be part of a town hall to debut the new logo and brand during the weekend of our annual Hero Dog Awards. We flew all of our Washington, D.C., and remote staff to Los Angeles to be with our colleagues there. About 95 percent of our employees attended the town hall, the unveiling of the new logo, and then the awards ceremony, which was taped for later broadcast on Hallmark Channel. Everyone received new branded shirts, hats, and pins; it was an incredible kickoff.

As a part of the brand rollout during the 2017 Hero Dog Awards weekend, we built a set that looked like a morning television show and called it "Good Morning with Robin and Jack." We actually modeled it after *Live with Kelly and Ryan*. I played Kelly Ripa, and our chief operating officer, Jack Hubbard, played Ryan Seacrest. We wanted to have some fun and to make our brand announcement memorable for our team. I think everyone got a big kick out of it. Instead of a bunch of suits on stage with a PowerPoint, we walked through the rebranding in a lighthearted but serious way.

We didn't forget that, first and foremost, our primary cheerleaders are our own staff and board members. It was the first time the entire employee base had been brought together, and the town hall was a time of great excitement around our brand launch. We even debuted our new Los Angeles rescue truck, which also featured the new branding. This truck completed my dream and vision for the expansion of the rescue program, which was to have a rescue truck and cache of resources in all the disaster-prone FEMA areas. The addition of the LA truck was the icing on the cake of our rescue program, making it truly national.

Jack Hubbard played a vital leadership role in our comprehensive rebranding effort. That included everything: our logo, the wraps on all of our vehicles, all of our digital properties, and a complete redo of our website, which was cumbersome and outdated. We've really grown e-philanthropy in a significant way; it has become a major leg on the stool. Its revenue streams, year after year, continue to grow. It's been an effective strategy for us.

As a part of our rebranding effort, we also, of course, made a big, splashy announcement to the world:

> **American Humane, America's first national humane organization, is celebrating 139 years of service with a rebranding effort that begins with changing the organization's name from American Humane Association to American Humane. The name change was accompanied by a new website, a new logo, and new slogan "First to Serve." In an exciting twist, on the same day the**

branding was unveiled, Ellen DeGeneres announced on her talk show that she was partnering with Walmart to contribute $500,000 to American Humane to support its animal rescue efforts in Louisiana.[27]

## The challenge: *Another view*

American Humane COO Jack Hubbard helped direct the rebranding effort. Here is his perspective on the challenge:

> Before I worked at American Humane, I knew them primarily from their farm program. I knew they operated the largest farm animal welfare program, and I saw their American Humane Certified logo on egg cartons at grocery stores. When I joined the organization, I soon realized there were even more programs than I had originally thought. From a donor perspective, it was a bit confusing. American Humane did and continues to do great work in so many different areas, from rescuing animals to improving conditions for farm and zoo animals and even training service dogs for veterans. But it was difficult to communicate all this in a simple way, and the old website didn't allow visitors to clearly understand American Humane at the macro level or clearly outline programs.
>
> From a marketing and fundraising viewpoint, this was one of the biggest challenges. American Humane seemed to be suffering from an embarrassment of riches.

*continued*

27  https://www.americanhumane.org/press-release/after-139-years-of-saving-animals-american
-humane-launches-new-branding-and-website/

There seemed to be almost too many programs with too many different names. The very richness and diversity of our work had become a liability and made it harder for people to pinpoint exactly who we were or what we did. And when you're not focused, you are not clear or concise. The key was simplifying our message and finding what was common to all of our work. That's where we came up with the "First to Serve" tag. That was white space that was not claimed by any other humane group.

We were and remain the first to protect animals in so many different areas . . . those in our homes and communities, agriculture, television and film, conservation centers, in transit, and so much more. We unified the messaging under the "First to Serve" umbrella and, equally important, threw the old website in the trash. We deleted 95 percent of the content and started over. Our goal was to create something that was aesthetically and logically clear and simple. I think we did just that. We also did an analysis of our donors to understand who they are and what demographics they represent and what messages they would respond to. Did they own dogs, cats, or both? We started fundraising and digital outreach programs that were customized to specific programs and demos and saw the response rate and donations increase. We also dedicated investment dollars to recruiting more monthly donors who are reliable supporters of our work. Rebranding, when done right, and with the correct follow-up can work wonders and raise real dollars for the mission.

## COMMUNICATING THE BRAND

Once you've got your brand sorted out, you've got to take the next big step, which is to communicate it. All the great branding in the world—all the high-paid marketing consultants, all the focus groups, all the time spent reflecting and refining—won't do you any good if you fail to communicate your brand to the people who might want to buy what you've got to sell. As I said, in my experience, it's best to use brains instead of brawn—to use marketing dollars wisely and to target potential customers selectively.

As part of our effort to reach large audiences with lifesaving humane education information and to save precious donor dollars for programs directly working to help improve the lives of animals and veterans in need, American Humane began creating high-quality but inexpensive public service campaigns. We produced highly effective campaigns for TV and radio featuring a variety of stars including Ice-T, Vivica A. Fox, Kristen Chenoweth, Jeff Corwin and Jack Hanna, among others. These PSAs have reached millions of people with important humane messages.

In addition, in 2019, American Humane launched a national billboard PSA campaign in partnership with the Outdoor Advertising Association of America, providing powerful humane messages about the importance of animals in our lives via thousands of electronic and conventional billboards across the country.

## PICK YOUR BATTLES: VALUE INNOVATION AS A TOOL FOR DIFFERENTIATION

In 1933, Harvard professor Edward Chamberlin first publicly unveiled the idea of product differentiation in his book *The Theory of Monopolistic Competition*. Differentiation today remains a key concept in marketing.

If you have a product that is differentiated in the marketplace and that stands out from the rest of the pack, you have a golden opportunity to garner more sales for the product than your competition. Not only that, but you also have the opportunity to command a higher price for the product. The result is increased revenue. In many cases—particularly if you are an early mover into a category—it allows you to insulate yourself from competitive infringement.

For decades, Volvo staked out unique turf for itself in the auto industry: the world's safest car. The conventional wisdom in the industry used to be that you couldn't talk about safety, because doing so might remind customers they could die in a car crash. Instead, the industry as a whole talked about anything but safety (shining the spotlight on snazzy new tail fins, hot new colors, and bigger and faster engines).

Volvo saw this as an opportunity to differentiate itself from the rest of the auto industry. The company didn't just talk about safety; it owned it and was able to command a premium for its products. Even today—at a time when the majority of car manufacturers now include safety in their product pitches—if you ask most any potential car buyer what car stands for safety, you'll get this answer: "Volvo."

In their book *Blue Ocean Strategy*, authors W. Chan Kim and Renée Mauborgne introduced the idea of value innovation as the cornerstone of blue ocean strategy. According to Kim and Mauborgne,

> **Value innovation is the simultaneous pursuit of differentiation and low cost. Value innovation focuses on making the competition irrelevant by creating a leap of value for buyers and for the company, thereby opening up new and uncontested market space. Because value to buyers comes from the offering's utility minus its price and because value to the company is generated from the offering's price minus its cost, value innovation is achieved only when the whole system of utility, price, and cost is aligned.**

Opening up the uncontested space—the blue ocean—as Kim and Mauborgne promote, requires suspending your own beliefs of what customers want and digging deep to find out what customers really want.

In a *Harvard Business Review* article, Kim and Mauborgne cited the example of a French hotel chain—Accor—that completely transformed its business by innovating around what its cost-conscious customers valued. According to the authors, some years ago, most French hotels fell into one of two categories. The first category comprised inexpensive hotels that provided noisy rooms with poor beds. The second category comprised more-expensive hotels that were quiet and offered quality beds and other amenities.

By listening to the wants of its customers, Accor turned the French hotel industry on its head, creating a completely new category of hotel that was inexpensive while offering high-quality accommodations. The strategy necessitated a complete ground-up redesign of Accor's hotels, boosting the elements most important to customers (room silence, bed quality, room cleanliness) and reducing (room size, receptionist) or eliminating altogether (restaurant, closets) the elements that customers cared about least.

To differentiate your brand, you need to turn the right knobs; that is, you need to follow a clear process for knowing exactly where to differentiate and then for innovating responses that will have the greatest impact. This process is not random, and it's definitely not something you can leave to chance. At American Humane, we did not leave to chance the safe treatment of animals that drive our programs and our impact. The right knobs for our rebrand were based on historical strengths rooted in solid science and evidence-based practices for animal protection. We defined what it is to be humane for animals in all environments. We are differentiated by offering innovative humane solutions, creating systematic change, and showing a demonstrable and measurable impact.

Much like a nonprofit in the crowded charitable space, Choice Hotels—which owns the Comfort Inn, Quality Inn, and Econo Lodge brands—was recently looking for a way to differentiate itself in the crowded field of low-cost lodging. In this category, it's typical for basic customer expectations not to be met—there's hair in the bed or the tub, or a light bulb is burned out, or the television remote control is missing. So Choice Hotels decided that the best way to set itself apart in this industry segment's sea of sameness was to focus on doing the basics better than its competitors, to ensure that its rooms are clean and in good condition and that everything is working as it is supposed to.

However, rather than simply making a list of the assumed basics that needed to be addressed and sending it out to the company's franchisees, Choice followed a methodical process for determining what was most important in the customers' eyes. Choice first looked at how people judged the condition of a room and then designed a program around those characteristics so that franchisees could actually go in and improve the condition of their rooms. Choice offered training films, job aids, metrics, inspections, and a compliance program—an entire program to help franchisees differentiate their hotels from the competition by executing the basics well.

When it comes right down to it, standing out in a crowded marketplace is a straightforward proposition. This, of course, doesn't make it any easier to execute whether you are running a charity or a hotel chain. Standing out requires discipline, it requires focus, and it requires innovation on the part of your people. Here are four things you can do right now to stand out the right way:

- Execute on the basics. Like Choice Hotels, determine what your customers' key expectations are, then deliver them without fail—day in and day out. For American Humane, our basics are animal protections.

- Offer something other people don't but that customers care about. JetBlue Airlines provides things that, for many years, other airlines did not, including televisions with free cable channels in each seatback and seating with more legroom. People don't fly the airline because of their on-time record, which is pretty good, or because they lose passenger bags less often than the competition. They fly JetBlue because the planes and the people who staff them are a little nicer. Their prices are pretty good too. American Humane offers humane solutions for animals in entertainment, on farms and ranches, and in zoos and aquariums. Consumers care about humane treatment, but other charities do not provide these solutions.

- Offer the same quality for less money. With its "everyday low prices," Walmart is famous for offering a wide variety of name-brand products at prices that are consistently lower than the competition's. For people who are pinching pennies, this is a very attractive value proposition. At American Humane, we've achieved an extremely high efficiency rate, with 91 cents of every dollar spent going directly into programs—ensuring our charitable ratings are stellar.

- Add a coolness factor to your low-priced offerings. A high-design, low-cost option, such as that offered by Target, is also a good way to stand out in a crowded marketplace. Although "coolness" is not something I am seeking at American Humane, we are standing out in a crowded marketplace with meaningful, sophisticated solutions that are efficient and, importantly, effective for the animals in our care.

## KEY TAKEAWAYS

- Keep your brand fresh and relevant.
- Use the brand wheel to get to the essence of who you are as an organization.
- Find the white space that your competitors don't occupy.
- Announce your new brand both internally and externally.

## VOICES FOR AMERICAN HUMANE
## ARIEL WINTER

If you're anything like me, your pets are not only your best friends; they're part of your family. So when disaster strikes, you want to be prepared to protect them.

Be sure to microchip or tag your pets. *Never* leave them behind in a major crisis, and be sure to have an emergency kit ready in your home at all times, with a pet crate or carrier, leash, blanket, ID and medications, their water bowl, and 7–10 days' worth of food.

American Humane, which has been rescuing animals for more than 100 years, has lifesaving tips that could make a *big* difference before, during, and after disasters such as hurricanes, tornadoes, floods, and wildfires.

To find out how to protect your entire family during a disaster and to help our best friends in their worst times, please visit AmericanHumane.org.

## VOICES FOR AMERICAN HUMANE
## ICE-T

As a veteran, I know that, for many former service men and women, the battle doesn't always end when they come home. Every day, 184 veterans are diagnosed with post-traumatic stress. And, sadly, 20 take their own lives. When nothing else helps, professionally trained service dogs can.

American Humane, serving the US military for over 100 years, rescues animals in need of forever homes and trains them to become free, lifesaving service dogs for our nation's veterans.

If you're a veteran or know a veteran struggling with post-traumatic stress or traumatic brain injury, please go to AmericanHumane.org to learn about their Pups4Patriots service dog program.

Let's give our veterans a fighting chance.

## WANT TO SAVE THE EARTH?
### Start with Your Local Zoo

The death last month of the world's last remaining male northern white rhinoceros was a red flag for the conservation movement and animal lovers everywhere. It was just the latest reminder of the precarious state of major fauna around the world: There are roughly 1,700 species of mammals, birds, reptiles, amphibians, or fish that are critically endangered.

Today is Earth Day, which raises awareness about how human actions such as pollution and overdevelopment threaten biodiversity. It presents an opportunity to reflect on the extinction of majestic creatures with whom we once shared the Earth and consider ideas to prevent further species loss.

Earth Day 2018 is focused on ending plastic pollution, particularly the single-use plastics that often end up in our oceans and waterways. The plastic threat to wildlife has been driven home by a recent viral video, viewed over 21 million times, of a straw being removed from the nose of a sea turtle. (This video

*continued*

is graphic and contains explicit language.) It's difficult to watch and not reflect upon the next time you're slurping a milkshake.

But there's something more proactive that Americans can do to celebrate Earth Day besides refusing a plastic straw the next time they're ordering at a restaurant or bar. They can support their local zoos and aquariums, which act as modern-day arks of hope for endangered animals across the world.

Zoos and aquariums offer a lifeline to animals who have inspired wonder for generations but have little-to-no natural habitat left. These include the most iconic zoo animals—such as big cats, primates, and pandas. Dozens of animals, including the South China tiger, no longer exist in the wild and are only kept in existence because of human care.

By saving species, zoos and aquariums also preserve the indescribable connection between people and animals, which has inspired generations of the young and young at heart. If this bond is frayed, it will doom endangered species. To generate support for conserving animals, people must first love animals. And to love animals, people must know them. Increasing urbanization means zoos and aquariums are the only opportunity most people get to knowing threatened animals. More than 183 million people—roughly half of the U.S. population—visit a zoo or aquarium annually.

Safe in zoos, critically endangered species can work to rebuild their populations, with the help of trained zoologists and breeders. Several species have been saved and reintroduced to the wild through zoo breeding programs. The Arabian oryx, whooping crane, black-footed ferret, and California condor have all seen their populations begin to recover as a result of zoos' efforts. Washington DC's National Zoo helped increase the population of the golden lion tamarins from about 200 to 3,200 in the wild today.

Zoos and aquariums also help finance conservation efforts, spending hundreds of millions of dollars annually on research efforts in breeding, habitat, and veterinary science. The World Association of Zoos and Aquariums has urged zoos to devote at least 3% of their budgets to conservation work. Most zoos have Earth Day programming today to help raise awareness of their inhabitants' plight.

To do the most good, zoos and aquariums must be held to the highest standards of animal welfare. American Humane's conservation program furthers this goal by certifying that animals in participating zoos and aquariums are healthy, positively social, active, safe, and living with proper light, sound, air, and heat levels. These standards are set by animal science experts, providing the third-party validation of humane treatment and positive welfare that an increasingly discerning public is demanding.

Some of the issues raised by Earth Day seem as vast as the million-square-mile mass of discarded plastics currently floating in the Pacific Ocean. But supporting local zoos and aquariums is a tangible step that has real benefits in protecting endangered species and helping prevent the next white rhino from disappearing from the planet.[28]

---

28  http://fortune.com/2018/04/22/earth-day-2018-ocean-plastic-pollution-zoo-aquarium/

# Funding a Better World

"The tipping point is that magic moment when an idea, trend, or social behavior crosses a threshold, tips, and spreads like wildfire."

—**Malcolm Gladwell,** *The Tipping Point*

**N**onprofits do a lot of good in the world, but they can only do good if they are financially viable and stable. If they run out of money, can't pay their staff, or leave bills unpaid, they will quickly become distracted from their work to just stay afloat on a day-to-day basis. Eventually, if they are unable to turn around their finances and get back on firm footing, the organization will shut its doors.

When I arrived at American Humane, we were not doing well. I'll never forget an exchange I had with a board member at my very first board meeting in February 2011. He took me aside and asked, "How much is it going to cost to shut this place down?" I sat back and I thought, "I can't believe that he would have the gall to bring me into this mess—*his* mess—and expect me to clean it up for him."

Based on our financial performance at the time, the board would have been well within its rights to close the doors and call it done. For fiscal year 2009, they had total expenses of $25.8 million on just $13.6 million in total revenue—resulting in a deficit of $12.2 million. The next two fiscal years were almost as bad:

| FY | Revenue | Expenses | Deficit |
|------|---------|----------|----------|
| 2010 | $15.7M | $21.6M | ($5.9M) |
| 2011 | $15.7M | $24.4M | ($8.7M) |

In my February 2011 report to the board, which set the stage for our transformation, I laid out a roadmap for how we would turn around American Humane before it sank entirely—or at least before board members like the one who asked me how much it would cost to shut down the organization decided to pull the plug. It was a turnaround situation, one that would require actions on the expense side and a disciplined focus on revenue generation. Together, we would make these tough decisions and execute them.

It was the board chair's job to help change the mindset of our board, and it was my job to do the hard work of actually changing the organization. That was the deal we made: He would run interference for me while I dove into the fray.

I set two goals for American Humane:

- Goal 1: Financial viability
- Goal 2: National awareness and strategic communications

Since both of these goals would require investment, I gathered together $1 million from our program and operations budgets and set it aside in what I called a "revenue generator fund." I knew that the $1 million was not going to solve all our problems, not by a long shot. But it was a step in the right direction. We didn't have the luxury of time to reflect on our situation. We had to turn on a dime to make a dime to cover salaries and keep the lights on.

My report was the first time the board had heard, in very plain terms, that we were in a turnaround situation. They certainly knew we were working under a deficit; they had approved deficit spending budgets for many years. But this was the first wakeup call for the board of directors that we weren't just experiencing a revenue problem; we were significantly over-shooting our expenses, as well. Revenue would have to be boosted, and spending would have to be stanched immediately for American Humane to avert bankruptcy. So change we did, but not before we experienced a tremendous amount of pain.

## TOUGH DECISIONS

Transforming American Humane wasn't easy. It was a lot of hard work over a long period of time for me and for my leadership team. During the first year in my position as CEO, no two days were the same. Each new day presented a new can of worms—or sometimes snakes—that would surprise and challenge us, but there was a mantra I followed that I learned from my father.

When I took on this job, I would talk with my father quite often about the newest problems that had popped up during the week. He would tell me, "Robin, you've got to dismiss all of that nonsense from your mind. The one thing that you need to do is bring revenue in every single day."

If you don't bring in revenue, then you won't be able to meet payroll; you won't be open for business. I would wake up every morning and ask myself, "What one thing can I do today to move forward revenue?" And when I went to bed at night, I would ask myself, "What did I achieve today to move forward revenue?" Revenue was my central focus. I had plenty of other things on my plate as CEO: the daily crises that inevitably arise for any organization, transforming our employee cul-ture, deciding what program tweaks needed to be made. All of that was important and required my attention, but it ultimately led back to the main question: "What can I do to drive revenue?" While I no longer have to ask that question every single day, I do ask it every week. It's still the mantra I live by.

Before I was hired, I had negotiated the option to move our head-quarters to Washington, D.C. This was an important move for us to make for a couple of different reasons. First, Denver was just too far out of the nonprofit mainstream, which tends to center in large metropolitan areas. Second, I wanted our organization to be physically close to Congress and the White House, so we could build better and stronger relationships with policymakers and our elected representatives.

At first, I thought we would maintain a program headquarters in Denver and a national headquarters in Washington. I soon realized, however, that our weak financials would not allow us to do that, so it would have to be one or the other. We simply couldn't afford both. We sold the Denver facility and used the funds to pay overdue bills and help keep the organization alive.

The board and I conducted a complete review of all our existing programs to determine which ones were contributing funds to our organization and which ones were draining away what precious funds we had remaining. In addition, the board approved a sizeable reduction in staff headcount. I knew we had great value and importance, but I also knew the organization had to be uplifted to survive and thrive. This wasn't weeding a garden but, rather, taking a backhoe to it.

After analyzing our programs, which we talked about in more depth earlier, the board agreed to remove child welfare from the mission statement. We instead put the focus on ensuring the welfare, wellness, and well-being of animals while unleashing the full potential of the bond between human and animals and the mutual benefit of that bond. That allowed us to really extract ourselves from a very expensive federal grant portfolio, and in 2012, start moving it to another nonprofit. Although many employees within the children's welfare team were understandably upset over this move, it was necessary to save American Humane.

When I arrived, we had about 160 employees. I didn't realize at the time that, to make our numbers work, we would have to lay off 60 percent of our staff. A large part of it was the children's welfare team, but we also had to pare staff in other parts of the organization. The layoffs hurt across all units, and it was challenging for me on an emotional level. I'm a mother and my family's breadwinner; I know the importance of each paycheck. But this institution simply could not survive a day longer as it was staffed.

The emotional toll was devastating, but I knew that if I didn't go through with these cost-saving measures, the institution would not be here to serve its mission for the next 100 years, so I kept that in my heart. Did we have value to offer a constituent who needed us? In our four new program planks, the answer was a resounding *yes*. We were the last moderate, science-based animal welfare group left. We had a mission to fulfill. We had the only historical legacy that needed to be honored by doing right by the mission, which meant a financial retraction in a grand way.

The decisions had been made before me to grow this institution using a deficit-spending model since 2006. I had to reverse that course with a gigantic retraction. That was a snake in a can that I had to take care of, and it would have been wrong of me not to have the moral courage to do so. It also would have been wrong of me to kick that can forward to the next generation of leadership. I had to do it, and I had to do it quickly.

The obstacles arrayed in front of me, however, were daunting. My biggest obstacles as the new CEO of American Humane were lack of good financial reporting information, lack of predictive cash flow modeling, and a fully loaded budget with large commitments in FY2011 and FY2012 as constructed by the previous administrations. The contracts—which included the federal grant contracts for child welfare, grossly inflated employment contracts, and numerous administrative and operational commitments—were not favorable to our revenue or expenses. As I pointed out to the board in my February 2012 report, not only did this situation pose a direct threat to the viability of American Humane, but it was putting our Charity Navigator ratings at risk.

Tough decisions were made, executed with integrity, and supported by the board. The entire staff worked without retirement benefits in 2012, and they personally absorbed travel expenses to help contribute to American Humane's financial goals. The staff made sacrifices across the board as the employee layoffs led to extra job duties and responsibilities. We were an organization going through a life-or-death transformation—one that would either sink American Humane or ensure its financial health for decades to come.

Over a period of two years, we accomplished the transformation by:

- Laying off more than 60 percent of our staff positions
- Reducing more than $16 million in budgeted expenses
- Ramping up external fundraising across all channels
- Recruiting key new hires to the leadership team
- Closing the Denver headquarters
- Transferring subsidized federal grants and contracts program to other entities
- Dealing with significant crisis communication issues
- Making over all areas of our operations and programs

The numbers tell the story. Here are our financial results for
FY2009–FY2019:

| Fiscal Year | Total Revenue | Total Expenses | Surplus/ (Deficit) |
|---|---|---|---|
| FY2009 | $13,639,055 | $25,820,602 | ($12,181,547) |
| FY2010 | $15,738,796 | $21,650,341 | ($5,911,545) |
| FY2011 | $15,748,350 | $24,425,797 | ($8,677,447) |
| FY2012 | $17,918,023 | $17,460,025 | $457,998 |
| FY2013 | $13,640,234 | $13,265,787 | $374,447 |
| FY2014 | $12,678,789 | $11,986,022 | $692,767 |
| FY2015 | $13,622,431 | $13,567,955 | $54,476 |
| FY2016 | $20,049,642 | $17,473,324 | $2,576,318 |
| FY2017 | $30,887,282 | $29,291,730 | $1,595,552 |
| FY2018 | $35,346,518 | $32,483,485 | $2,863,033 |
| FY2019 | $44,737,010 | $43,296,503 | $1,440,507 |

| RESOURCE UTILIZATION | | | |
|---|---|---|---|
| Fiscal Year | Programs | Fundraising | General Admin |
| FY2009 | 86.9% | 9.5% | 3.7% |
| FY2010 | 79.0% | 14.4% | 6.6% |
| FY2011 | 77.4% | 13.1% | 9.5% |
| FY2012 | 81.9% | 13.8% | 4.3% |
| FY2013 | 78.2% | 14.3% | 7.5% |
| FY2014 | 76.8% | 17.0% | 6.2% |
| FY2015 | 79.5% | 14.4% | 6.1% |
| FY2016 | 85.6% | 9.2% | 5.2% |
| FY2017 | 91.2% | 5.2% | 3.6% |
| FY2018 | 91.2% | 5.5% | 3.3% |
| FY2019 | 91.3% | 6.1% | 2.6% |

Since I took over as CEO, we increased our total revenue by 184 percent. As illustrated in the Resource Utilization chart, we did that while growing our commitment to programming and cutting administrative expenses. In FY2012, the first year I personally owned the budget, we ran our first surplus in years. Although revenues didn't increase much that year, we dramatically cut our expenses—by almost $7 million from the previous fiscal year. We reversed a deficit of almost $9 million in just a year, posting a modest surplus while honoring the inflated employment contracts made by the previous administration. It was no small accomplishment.

As I wrote in my report to the board in October 2012,

> **The financial condition was absolutely dire a year ago, caused by years of approved deficit spending resulting in a dramatic spend-down of the large bequest. Revenue as a percentage of expense ran from 68% down to a low of 58% with the interim CEO's budget and built-in heavy contractual burdens. Sustainability is simply not possible with conditions being what they were. And as we previously discussed, I was stunned to learn the depths of the financial condition and was in a very desperate position so soon after having started this position.**
>
> **That downward trend has now ended with the first operating surplus in many years, and the first positive change in net assets at the close of FY2012. Program expenses are 83%, and administrative/executive expenses kept minimal at 4.2%. The current ratio is good at 2:2. Revenue grew at 29% across the board over the prior year: fundraising revenue grew at 35% over the prior year and 101% since the recession hit in 2008 given the recent fundraising success.**

I had proven to the board—and to myself—that by getting back to the basics, we could transform our 100-plus-year-old organization. As we began to run surpluses instead of deficits, we found ourselves with a clean, level playing field to continue to advance our new administration's cost-cutting and efficiency measures while pursuing our new program platform for funding. That gave us much needed breathing room.

## EXPERIMENTING WITH NEW REVENUE

We tried lots of different revenue generating tactics at once because we needed all hands on deck just to bring in revenue. We talked for the first time ever about national signature events. We talked about how we could get foundations involved in our cause. I recognized early on that foundations would be a harder piece of our platform to build out because it's extremely difficult to go to a foundation when you show a track record of the kind of deficit budgets we had. For major corporate foundations and private family foundations, our record would not meet a litmus test for funding, and I had to explain that to the board.

We created a new mantra for the organization, "Fundraising is a team sport," which meant we would break down all barriers inside American Humane getting in the way of raising funds. At the time, fundraising for this institution was done by a small group in the Denver building who didn't actually have much opportunity to engage with programs. There were so many walls—proverbial, literal, and figurative—within American Humane. We had to break down those walls across programs, operations, and philanthropy in order to get some of these new ideas tested to see if they would work.

We brainstormed all sorts of ideas we hoped would better focus the team on our mission while at the same time generating buzz and serving as potential new funding sources for American Humane. We came up with a variety of ideas, including:

- A national partnership with The Weather Channel
- A Discovery Channel Profile series
- Research on canines and childhood cancer (funded by Zoetis)
- The Cat Welfare Forum
- The Animal Actors Summit
- The National Commission on People and Pets
- A citizen scientist business model
- The Hero Dog Awards

Although some of these ideas sprouted and blossomed, others died a quiet death. I knew, however, that the more good ideas we tried, the greater our chances would be that some would take hold and become important to American Humane in the future. Such was the case with the Hero Dog Awards.

The concept for the Hero Dog Awards came about right before I accepted the position of CEO in 2010. As soon as I realized the full extent of our financial troubles, I knew we needed to get creative—fast. There was no time for me to leisurely settle into my new position. The survival of American Humane required I hit the ground running, taking immediate and decisive action to get our organization out of the doldrums into which it had sailed.

In early 2011, we kicked off a six-month nationwide search for nominees for our first campaign. We received nominations for dogs from all 50 states, and the nominees received more than 500,000 votes from members of the public. It was an overwhelming response for a brand-new program.

After the votes were counted, our first national Hero Dog winner was selected: Roselle, a female Labrador Retriever. When you read the story of Roselle as told by her owner, Michael Hingson, I think you'll understand why she was the public's overwhelming choice for our first national Hero Dog Award:

> On September 11, 2001, my guide dog (for the blind),
> Roselle, and I were working in the World Trade Center
> on the 78th floor of Tower One when the airplane
> crashed into our building. From the outset, Roselle
> guided and did her job perfectly, as we went to the stair-
> well and traveled down 1,463 stairs. After leaving the
> building, we were across the street from Tower Two
> when it collapsed. Despite the dust and chaos, Roselle
> remained calm and totally focused on her job, as debris
> fell around us and even hit us. We found a subway
> entrance, where we could escape the heavy dust. All

**that day, Roselle worked flawlessly. She saved my life and truly is the greatest dog hero of all.**

What Michael didn't mention is that not only did Roselle lead *him* safely down the 1,463 steps from the 78th floor of the World Trade Center Tower One to the street below on that terrible day, but Roselle also led 30 *other* people down Stairwell B along with Michael, taking more than an hour to complete their harrowing journey. Sadly, Roselle died in June 2011, and Michael accepted her award posthumously.

The production and broadcast of the American Humane Hero Dog Awards was a pivotal moment for an organization that was running on fumes with two flat tires. The television show allowed us to reintroduce American Humane to the world using the power of television, storytelling, and the human–animal bond. It became an early win for us financially.

Our success with the Hero Dog Awards continues to this day. On October 5, 2019, we hosted the ninth annual American Humane Hero Dog Awards gala at the legendary Beverly Hilton hotel in Los Angeles. Our Hero Dog Awards is an annual, nationwide campaign that identifies and recognizes ordinary dogs that have done extraordinary things. Whether it's saving lives on the battlefield, lending sight or hearing to a human companion, or simply providing the tail-wagging welcome a weary pet owner relishes at the end of a hard day, there can be no doubt at all that the bond between dogs and people is a remarkably strong one.

Dogs compete for awards in seven different categories: Law Enforcement Dogs, Service Dogs, Therapy Dogs, Military Dogs, Search and Rescue Dogs, Guide/Hearing Dogs, and Shelter Dogs, who repay (and even rescue) their owners for rescuing them. After voting by the American public is completed, winners in each category are flown to Hollywood with their human friends to attend the American Humane Hero Dog Awards gala. There, they walk the red carpet surrounded by crowds of "pupparazzi" from major media outlets, are recognized in video tributes broadcast during the two-hour national television show in the fall, receive their Hero Dog category award statue, and mingle with America's top celebrities—both the two-legged and four-legged variety.

This event gave us hope for the future. We knew that our decision to whittle down our programs from more than 40 to just four program planks was the right one. Our newfound organizational focus was attracting the kind of donors that had the financial wherewithal to help us dig out of the very deep hole that had been dug for us. Increased revenue combined with decreased expenses gave us a very big shovel to start digging ourselves out.

## FINANCIAL STABILITY

As we began to break down the walls that divided us, we pulled together full force into our revenue diversity platform, which brought us some success—and a glimmer of hope in some very dark times for American Humane. Everything that we'd been working toward—defining our mission, rethinking our programs, hiring the best leaders, growing a positive culture, and claiming our brand—finally coalesced. The long days, longer nights, and seemingly endless crises were finally paying dividends. Soon, I knew American Humane would be around, doing good and doing well, for the long haul.

Exactly one year after I became CEO, on the stage at the Hero Dog Awards, we received our first million-dollar check from a living donor— the philanthropist Lois Pope. Lois's remarkably generous donation was the spark that transformed our giving platform, which, at that time, averaged just $250 for major gifts. Then, when we closed the first fiscal year in June 2012—the first fiscal year for which I had budget responsibility—we produced an operating surplus of $457,998 on $17.9 million in revenue, our first surplus in seven years.

That's when I knew we could do it. We were on the right course.

## REWARDING EMPLOYEES

As our financial health increased, we were gradually able to boost employee salaries and benefits—boosting employee morale, engagement, and productivity all at the same time. In addition, we agreed to continue to subsidize healthcare coverage to the tune of 90 percent of individual health insurance plans and 70 percent of family health insurance plans.

Here are some comments from American Humane employees whose commitment to the organization was strengthened as the benefits of a stronger financial position flowed down to them:

> "I know budgets are tight, and I can't tell you how much it means to receive this appreciation. Both the salary increase and the new position mean a lot to me from a personal accomplishment standpoint, and I am very grateful for the recognition and continued opportunities you provide. Thank you, thank you, thank you!!!"
>
> —Amy, Humane Research

> "I greatly appreciate the raise and recognition! I promise to fulfill my new responsibilities effectively. Thank you so much for trusting in my capabilities."
>
> —Claudia, Humane Hollywood

> "Thank you! I truly appreciate being appreciated, and I will give my best to not only meet but strive toward surpassing the level of trust, dedication, and professionalism requested by this organization and deserved by those I have contact with internally as well as those I have exchanges with outside of American Humane. Thank you again. It is truly a pleasure to be a member of the American Humane family!"
>
> —Robert, Accounting

Although employees could see the benefits of change directly affecting them, there's one more thing that the turnaround did for them: It filled them with a tremendous sense of pride in American Humane and our mission of saving animals.

In just one example, our first annual Hero Dog Awards became a media sensation while showcasing some very inspiring dogs and their remarkable stories. We attracted more than 1 million YouTube video views and more than 6.6 million Facebook page views, and more than 500,000 unique votes were cast by members of the public (we more than doubled that number—to over 1.2 million votes—the very next year). In addition, we signed on 32 celebrity supporters as judges and presenters and 18 charity partners. We were all proud that we were able to bring the stories of these dog heroes to life—and to the attention of the public.

Another source of pride for our team was our new celebrity support-ers—well-known animal lovers who felt a great affinity for the American Humane mission and became involved in supporting our work. Among those notables are Betty White, Whoopi Goldberg, Jay Leno, Billy Crystal, Shirley MacLaine, Quentin Tarantino, Ellen DeGeneres, Naomi Judd, Richard Gere, Ariel Winter, Kristin Chenoweth, Vivica A. Fox, Emmanuelle Vaugier, Miranda Lambert, Pauley Perrette, Katharine McPhee, Martin Short, Peter Fonda, Mickey Rooney, Ice-T, Jack Hanna, Jeff Corwin, Allison Sweeney, Barbara Niven, Joey Lawrence, John Ondrasik, Candy Spelling, Michelle Forbes, Victoria Stilwell, Carolyn Hennesy, Edie McClurg, and many others. Betty White, a for-mer board member, graciously participated in a fundraising commercial for American Humane, along with a CrowdRise campaign for social media fundraising.

As we closed out 2014 and prepared to kick off 2015, every indica-tion was that our change initiative was not only achieving its goals; it was going to stick. We had racked up three consecutive years of oper-ating surpluses, along with three years of increases in net assets. We were top rated by Charity Watch and given a gold rating by GuideStar. All programs were operating on their bottom lines for the first time ever, with new business models and funding streams in place. Our work generated more than *20 billion* media impressions in 2014—including top-tier news agencies such as BBC, *Fox and Friends*, the *Today Show*, *USA Today*, NPR, CNN, and the Associated Press. By 2019, we were generating 150,000 media pieces a year.

I believe the wisdom of our change initiatives and the courage of our staff, executives, and board in executing them were instrumental to their success. We created a new culture—in essence, a new community—for our staff, our board, our supporters, and our stakeholders to inhabit. As Malcolm Gladwell once wrote, "If you want to bring a fundamental change in people's belief and behavior, you need to create a community around them, where those new beliefs can be practiced and expressed and nurtured."

## KEY TAKEAWAYS

- For an organization to do good in the world, it's got to do well financially.

- All programs should be fully funded, pulling their own weight.

- Focus on ways to drive revenue every day that align with your mission.

- Step into new spaces and become creative with fundraising.

- If a product, service, or program can't support itself, then either increase your investment, or let it go.

- Make the tough decisions necessary to ensure the long-term financial health and sustainability of your organization.

- Know your run rate cold and focus on bringing in revenue every day.

- Practice transformational leadership.

# VOICES FOR AMERICAN HUMANE
## JACK HUBBARD

Jack Hubbard joined American Humane in 2016, first serving as chief marketing officer and then moving into the position of chief operating officer. Jack's previous experience was in the private sector, working at a national public relations firm and before that for UBS Wealth Management. This background provided Jack with a firm foundation of real-world business experience that he brought with him to American Humane.

We asked Jack to explain what first attracted him to the organization and what it is that separates American Humane from other nonprofits.

> I come from the private sector, and I liked that American Humane was run professionally in a manner where the expectation was that programs should be self-sustaining and that revenue-generating positions in the fundraising area were expected to raise multiple times their costs. When I became familiar with American Humane, I realized that it was different than other nonprofits in culture and leadership. Robin expected philanthropy team members to be raising multiple times their salaries, which I wholeheartedly agreed with and was tasked with ensuring. After all, when there is no margin, there is no mission. We needed our philanthropy and communications teams to work side by side to raise more dollars to support our lifesaving work.
>
> Ultimately, we ended up rebuilding the whole philanthropy team from the ground up and recruited a new group of people—some who didn't even have philanthropy backgrounds. Some even came from

corporate sales environments. They had the drive and the motivation we were looking for, and they got us the results we were looking for.

## PET LOVE:
### An Antidote to America's Stress

Sadly, we're global leaders in feeling agitated—there are only three countries in the world that are more stressed out than the United States.

But there's an antidote . . . a healthy dose of pet love. To remedy some of the anxiety plaguing America, individuals should cultivate and nurture bonds with animals. Those bonds, in addition to reducing stress in America, will inspire people to live humane lifestyles and build a more humane world.

Engaging with, owning, and loving animals is a proven remedy for the stress of the workaday world. When people are in a stressful situation, the hormone cortisol spikes in the body, making it a useful tool for measuring stress. Interaction with animals is proven to lower both cortisol levels and blood pressure, according to the National Institutes of Health. In other words, science backs up what many people know intuitively—they feel better after petting a dog or cat.

Beyond reducing stress, bonding with animals offers a multitude of benefits.

Consider the effects of adding a pet to a family. Families with dogs are more likely to engage in activities together and their children are more likely to be visited by friends. And for couples whose children have recently moved out of the house, owning a pet leads to better mental and physical health.

But pets don't just bring advantages to families. Adding pets to schools, for example, can be beneficial. Through a partnership with Pet Care Trust, we studied the effects of introducing animals into the classroom. Teachers reported that having a class pet improved both classroom social interactions and class participation while decreasing behavioral issues in the classroom.

Or consider the benefits of animal-assisted therapy (AAT) for a variety of patient groups. AAT helps elderly patients with schizophrenia take care of themselves and interact with society. And researchers have found that AAT in long-term care facilities is particularly useful at generating longer conversations and interactions between residents. For children with autism, including a dog in occupational therapy treatment helps patients use more language and engage in more social interaction.

The bond between people and animals offers innumerable benefits—including reduced stress. Out of that bond flows love and respect for animals. People who recognize the importance of animals also realize how important it is to treat them with kindness.

At the organization I lead, American Humane, we're promoting Be Kind to Animals Week this week, the oldest commemorative week in U.S. history and the nation's longest-running humane education campaign. In fact, it has been our 143-year mission to ensure that animals—whether they are in homes, on farms, acting on movie sets or living in zoos and aquariums—are treated humanely.

Recognizing the importance of animals to our society, individuals can ensure that animals are treated well by committing

*continued*

to a humane lifestyle. People have a lot of power as consumers, and they can exercise that power to promote the humane treatment of animals by purchasing humanely raised food, visiting zoos and aquariums that are humanely certified, and watching movies that support animal welfare on set.

Animals can help America with our stress problem. They already enrich our lives in our homes, classrooms, and hospitals. In return, we owe it to them to ensure that all animals are treated humanely.[29]

---

29  https://www.foxnews.com/opinion/dr-robin-ganzert-pet-love-an-antidote-to-americas-stress

## HOW ZOOS AND AQUARIUMS CAN HELP SAVE 1 MILLION SPECIES FROM EXTINCTION

It's time for everyone who cares about preserving animal life to rally behind zoos and aquariums that act as modern arks of hope for many species.

Roughly 1 million plant and animal species are at risk of extinction, according to a recent United Nations assessment. As animals find it increasingly difficult to live in the wild, it's important to leverage the power of zoos and aquariums to protect animals and restore endangered species, even as some activists seek to dismantle these arks of hope.

The U.N. report paints a bleak picture—earth is becoming increasingly inhospitable thanks to irresponsible land and water use, climate change, pollution and other man-made causes.

Right now, zoos and aquariums should be rallying points for conservationists. Unfortunately, between 2007 and 2017, nearly a quarter of Americans became more opposed to zoos and aquariums, according to a YouGov poll.

And an activist group called Empty the Tanks is hosting a global series of aquarium protests Saturday demanding that all aquatic mammals be released into the sea. These so-called activists apparently aren't concerned with saving animal lives. The U.N. report revealed that more than a third of marine mammals are at risk of extinction.

Zoos and aquariums are tools by which we can preserve animal life while habitats are threatened. A child born today

*continued*

who reaches 80 years of age will live to see half of the world's current species become extinct, according to Elizabeth Kolbert, author of *The Sixth Extinction: An Unnatural History*.

Countless species are threatened by human activities such as pollution, overhunting, overfishing and habitat destruction.

## Managing the threat of extinction

Last month, the U.S. Fish and Wildlife Service announced it would consider classifying the giraffe as an endangered species. That's after wild giraffe populations fell by up to 40% over three decades. Giraffes may join the nearly 1,500 species of animals that are already considered endangered or threatened by the USFWS.

Fortunately, zoos are stepping up as sanctuaries for these iconic and beautiful animals. Giraffes living at Tanganyika Wildlife Park, located in Goddard, Kansas, have given birth to over 50 calves. That's important to keeping the species alive.

Last month, we also learned that Halley Bay, home to the world's second-largest colony of emperor penguins, just finished its third year of almost total breeding failure, according to a study in *Antarctic Science*, a publication of the Cambridge University Press.

And they're not the only penguins in trouble. The southern rockhopper penguin, which hails from rocky shores in the southern hemisphere—from New Zealand to Chile—is threatened. Luckily, the rockhopper penguin is one of the animals living and bred at SeaWorld Orlando, a refuge for these birds.

But not all activists see it that way. SeaWorld Orlando is one of the locations where Empty the Tanks is organizing a protest this week.

## Zoos, aquariums are arks of hope

In light of the U.N. report, it's time for activists, ordinary folks, politicians, and everyone in between to rally behind zoos and aquariums that act as modern arks of hope for many species, like penguins and giraffes.

Obviously, whenever animals live in human care, there can be bad actors. That's why we at American Humane launched the first-ever, independent, science-based, genuinely third-party humane certification program focused on animals in zoos and aquariums. We wanted families to know that the zoos and aquariums they visit are doing right by the animals in their care.

In fact, both SeaWorld and Tanganyika Wildlife Park have received certification from American Humane. Through a vigorous evaluation process, they are recognized by our organization as facilities with exceptional standards for the humane treatment of the animals in their care.

The sixth mass extinction of animal and plant life on earth is accelerating, making it necessary to involve people in the conservation of earth's animals. Animals like penguins and giraffes are counting on us. For their sake, we need to support facilities that protect animal life against harsh environments. [30]

---

30  https://www.usatoday.com/story/opinion/2019/05/11/zoos-aquariums-can-help-save-one-million
-species-extinction-column/1152477001/

# Meeting the Future Head On

"Maybe it's animalness that will make the world right again: the wisdom of elephants, the enthusiasm of canines, the grace of snakes, the mildness of anteaters. Perhaps being human needs some diluting."

—Carol Emshwiller

For most of this book, we've talked about how to adapt, grow, and transform. We've discussed clawing your way out of a bad situation and setting yourself up for success. But once you're out of the pit, what then? Staying still is never an option. You have to identify areas for growth that align with your mission and that will strengthen your organization. For American Humane, it became clear where and how we should grow. We just had to look at the world around us and find where animals needed help.

## NEW PROBLEMS REQUIRE NEW SOLUTIONS

Scientists have issued a dire warning: We are currently in the middle of a devastating change to our planet, one that will continue to haunt us for centuries to come. This change is what is known as the *sixth mass extinction*, and it is believed to have resulted in a shocking loss of animal life over the past century. Research shows that up to half of all species—mammals, birds, reptiles, and amphibians—are heading toward oblivion by the year 2050. In the case of mammals alone, biologists report that species are being lost at a rate that is 20 to 100 times normal.[31]

Because this current mass extinction is believed to be the result of human behavior—and not of an asteroid impact, volcanic activity, or other natural phenomena like those that likely triggered previous extinctions— if we are able to change our behavior as humans, it may be possible to reverse its effects.

I always like to reference the saying, "You can't protect what you don't love, and you can't love what you don't know." Zoos and aquariums are vitally important to people, animals, and the world we share, but the sector has faced incredible public pressures due to the narrative of animals in captivity. I had often wondered where our next generation of conservationists would come from if zoos and aquariums were forced to shut down. Who would care to fight for the real voiceless—the animals in the wild—when there is no wild left?

I was asked by several leaders in the zoo and aquarium community to meet at a restaurant. The restaurant was dark inside, which turned out to be very fitting. This was in the wake of the documentary film *Blackfish*, which shined an unflattering light on SeaWorld's killer whale program. The film was devastating for SeaWorld. As a result of all the negative publicity, the park suffered a significant decline in attendance, along with a multimillion-dollar financial loss. People's faith in keeping animals in human care was shaken. It was no surprise that the zoo and aquarium community wanted to meet with me.

Over dinner, I shared with them the success of our American Humane certification programs for animals in film and television and on farms. I told them how our programs continued to expand and about the tremendously positive impact they were having on animals across our nation and

---

31  https://www.washingtonpost.com/news/morning-mix/wp/2015/06/22/the-earth-is-on-the-brink
-of-a-sixth-mass-extinction-scientists-say-and-its-humans-fault/?noredirect=on&utm_term
=.ceb2968ef0eb

around the world. After a while, someone stopped me mid-conversation. He said,

> Robin, the reason we have you here is that we have a very simple request. We would like for you to create rigorous certification programs for zoos and aquariums just like you have done for farms, just like you have in Hollywood, because we need your help. We need that independent third-party assurance for moms and dads, for families, to come back to the aquarium, back to the zoo. We need them to recognize that we really do provide humane treatment for animals in our care. We need to save species, change lives, and promote conservation.

In many cases, the animals in zoos and aquariums are on the endangered species list, and these organizations are truly dedicated to protecting them and finding ways to increase their numbers in the wild. These are the incredible animals that you would not see in your own hometown if the zoo and aquarium did not exist. Children wouldn't have the opportunity to see these animals up close and in person. This was a heavy mantle of responsibility that they wanted American Humane to bear. They wanted us to step forward with moral courage to define what it was to be humane for animals in human care, to help ensure and verify those conditions, and then to share those values with the families who were reluctant to return to their hometown zoo or aquarium.

After the meeting in that darkly lit restaurant, I immediately got on the phone with our board chair. I told him, "We have a very real opportunity. It's not going to be without some criticism. It's going to take a lot of moral courage to step up and be a friend of those zoos and aquariums that actually do things right." I knew we could do it, and we could do it well. But would the board wish us to go on this journey?

We knew how to build a humane certification model. We had proved our expertise in doing that time and time again, uplifting the care of animals in our lives. But, given the post-*Blackfish* climate, I knew that we would be putting the organization at risk for negative publicity. This is not about publicity, good or bad; it's about doing what's best for the animals.

John Payne, our board chair, said, "Wherever animals are, American Humane needs to be there. It is our moral and ethical responsibility and cause for action to do this. We must do this."

As I said, you can't protect what you don't love, and you can't love what you don't know. And we want good zoos and aquariums to be recognized as the arks of hope that they are for the world's remarkable species and those facing extinction.

We decided to commit resources to create a completely independent, science-based certification program for zoos and aquariums. It would take funding, however, and at that point, it wasn't yet clear where that would come from.

Just three short weeks later, I was given an opportunity to speak to 200 members of the Alliance of Marine Mammal Parks and Aquariums. This is a group of institutions in North America that have marine mammals in their care. Would they be supportive of the creation of an independent third-party certification program for the world's zoos and aquariums?

I got in there, and I thought, in front of these 200 people, I could either do a standard PowerPoint slide show or I could tell a story. So, I got up there and told my story:

> I have three wonderful children. When my son Robert was in kindergarten, at age five, he came home that very first day with his new business card. The business card was a fun way of telling their mom and dad what the kids were going to be when they grew up.
>
> My son's friends went home with all the business cards you would expect—firefighter, doctor, policeman, teacher. Robert's teacher was rather stunned,

because Robert said, "I want to be a dolphin trainer!" His teacher had to quickly create a special dolphin trainer business card for him, because he had to go home with a laminated business card when school ended that day. So at age five, Robert presented his business card to me, and he told me he was going to be a dolphin trainer when he grew up.

When my son turns 21, will there even be an opportunity for him to become a dolphin trainer? This industry has faced so much criticism lately, most of it not rooted in science or fact. Now, here's the big question before you today: Are you going to band together and tell your own stories, or are you going to let others own that narrative? Because, at the end of the day, children like Robert may not be able to have their kindergarten dreams come true. There may no longer be a need for any dolphin trainers—period.

I offered them an opportunity to step up and do the right thing to ensure that zoos and aquariums were inspiring and teaching the next generation of conservationists and would still be open to the public. We had to ensure that animals would have an opportunity to be protected by these great institutions, which have saved so many species, and that dolphin training would still be a job in the next 10 or 20 years.

After I completed my presentation, I had the support of many passionate animal lovers who believed they were treating the animals in their care well and were willing to subject their practices to a rigorous examination based on science, not just emotion, to prove it. The results of our new effort are heartening. Just two and a half years after we launched our new American Humane Conservation program, 60 of the world's top zoos and aquariums are now independently audited by animal experts and certified by American Humane. Today, we have a presence on every continent except Africa and Antarctica. And it all started when Robert came home at age five wanting to be a dolphin trainer.

As our program continued to grow globally, we have taken the opportunity to do groundbreaking work in China. We were asked to lead the first-ever study of wild animals in zoos and aquariums throughout Asia and provide global best practices that have been defined by American Humane. We are now taking humane principles to another continent and sharing our science-based practices elevating the care and protection of animals.

Zoos and aquariums are vitally important not only in preserving disappearing species but also in educating the next generation of animal lovers, the next generation of conservationists, the next generation of those who are going to protect animals in all forms, in their own backyards and across the globe. The world is changing; we can't stop it, but we can help manage the change. That's what American Humane is doing. We're helping to manage the change for the benefit of millions of animals in our nation and all around the world.

## CREATING THE RIGHT PARTNERSHIPS

I'm a big believer in building partnerships with individuals and organizations that share your goals and values and those of your organization. When you build the right partnerships with the right individuals and organizations, the benefits to everyone involved can be tremendous. In the case of American Humane, building partnerships has brought us tremendous value while helping to elevate our national standing. In addition, the partnerships we have built help to inspire and create pride within our team, which was critically important as we brought change to most every aspect of our organization.

In just one example, I mentioned earlier our groundbreaking Canines and Childhood Cancer Study. As you may recall, the idea behind the study was to scientifically prove the anecdotal stories we have long heard that contact with animals can provide benefits to people with cancer—specifically, children.

As we considered the direction we should take with this important research, it quickly became clear that this was something we should not do on our own. Although we could have assembled and funded our own research team to conduct the study, we realized it would have a much greater impact if we created some key partnerships. These partnerships would help us assemble the very best researchers while providing greater visibility and perhaps even some additional funding. As we looked across the humane landscape, we decided that Zoetis—formerly the animal health business of Pfizer—would be the perfect partner, and indeed, they were. They supported the Canines and Childhood Cancer Study for seven years, from beginning to end. We quite literally could not have accomplished the tremendous outcomes we did without them.

I believe one of the most important things modern nonprofits can do is to find others who have common interests—likeminded individuals, foundations, and businesses—and then build alliances and partnerships. It's truly a case where 1 + 1 = 3. The whole is greater than the sum of its parts. Although we retain our independence, we are collaborative and open in the things that we do.

Some in the nonprofit world believe corporations and other businesses are an evil that should be avoided—the enemy. In my experience, this is definitely not the case. Although the primary mandate of businesses is to make money, corporations can be important partners in all sorts of initiatives. The key is determining which businesses to partner with, which ones will combine with you in ways that create the most value to your constituents and help you achieve your mission.

In just one example of many, we teamed up with Chicken Soup for the Soul Pet Food in 2018 to deliver 4,000 pounds of free premium food for animals displaced by California's deadly Camp Fire. This is in addition to our "Fill a Bowl . . . Feed a Soul" partnership, which allows us to provide more than one million meals annually to US animal shelters and pet food distribution centers that house, feed, and care for millions of animals each year. Corporate partnerships such as these have enabled us to extend our mission much further than we ever could by ourselves—saving the lives of thousands of animals while building morale within our staff and helping to solidify the changes we have made.

## A HOUSE DIVIDED CANNOT STAND

Making change part of the fabric of an organization is all about how successful you, as a leader, are in creating a compelling vision of the future and then getting your employees excited and inspired enough to join you on your journey. You can't force people to change; they won't. They have to want to change.

I've talked in this book about our sale of the Denver headquarters and our move to Washington, D.C. When I became CEO of American Humane, it just didn't make sense to me that our headquarters was in Denver. Although the building was nice enough, it was very isolated from the rest of the world, and its design was not conducive to building a cohesive team. The headquarters building was three floors tall, and it was shaped like an X, with two wings that formed each half of the X. Right away, I could see that the building itself physically separated and segregated two major divisions. We had the animal division on one side of the building and the children's division on the other side. We were taking our people and physically dividing them in half. This division within our headquarters made our change initiatives that much more difficult to institute.

I'm a big believer that stuff—our beautiful office building in Colorado and other physical assets we had at the time—is not the most important thing for an organization like ours—or, really, for any organization. The most important thing for American Humane is our human capital, our people.

The physical building was not important to our mission. So, we sold it and made the decision to move our headquarters to the nation's capital so that we could be a voice for the entire nation—not just the outskirts of Denver, where no one even knew we existed. Having all our leadership in one place would also enable us to meet together regularly, building teamwork and camaraderie. I could sit in a meeting with the people who were leading the Humane Conservation Program on one side of me and the people who were leading the American Humane Farm Program on the other. It was important to put the leadership together so that we started to see these are not all separate divisions.

We had to find our commonality of purpose and mission. It wasn't just "I only care about farm animals" or "I only care about seals" or "I only care about children with cancer." We wanted to make sure that the leadership team began to physically work next to one another. We ate together; we had meetings together. Being in close physical proximity was, itself, very important for building understanding and bonds within the team.

We brought the organization back together—into an organic whole, much as it was in American Humane's early days. And we managed the change by bringing our mission to life. When you engage your employees in your mission and make it real, it's a powerful thing.

When Hurricane Sandy devastated the East Coast of the United States in 2012, we took a team of employees to New York and New Jersey to help. We called up major pet food distributors and got a truckload of free food and free medicines from animal health organizations. We loaded up our giant trucks and got them ready for our journey. We all put on blue jeans and our American Humane shirts and hats—quite a different uniform for an administrative team that usually dresses in more formal office attire. Once we got on the road, we headed to one of the hardest hit shelters in Atlantic City.

People always think of the glitz and glamour of Atlantic City, but it is actually a very poor town, with 40.6 percent of the population living below the poverty line.[32] It's right on the ocean, probably no more than a yard or two above sea level, so it got hit really hard by Sandy. We visited a shelter where people were gathered in the aftermath of the storm. Unfortunately, the shelter did not allow people to bring their pets along, so if they couldn't

---

32  https://datausa.io/profile/geo/atlantic-city-nj

find someone to take care of them, the pets were often left behind. We met a child in the shelter who told us a very interesting story.

President Obama had visited the shelter in the aftermath of the storm. He introduced himself to the people gathered there, saying, "How are you doing? Is there anything we can do?"

When President Obama asked the child if there was anything he could do to help, the child replied, "Well, I'm fine, but I really need your help."

Obama asked, "What's the problem?"

The child said, "The problem is we left our two cats in our house, and the house is flooded. I'm afraid they're not going to live."

Obama ordered a Marine helicopter to check out the situation. It landed on the roof of the child's family's house, cut a hole through the roof, and went in to look for the cats. They found the two cats standing on a table that was floating in the house. They easily could have drowned. We called them the Obama cats. They meant so much to this child that he asked the president of the United States to intervene, and he did, rescuing the cats.

We were there, and we provided assistance to the young man and his family. We brought hundreds of thousands of pounds of food to the shelter for all these animals that had been displaced and did a good deed—together, as a team.

We do this work, and I do this work, because we believe in our mission; it's a mission-driven model. Each and every one of the employees at American Humane connects deeply into that mission; it's not a choice. We deliver on the outcomes of that mission because that's what we're called to do, and we gladly accept the call. But our first call to action in our early days was to ensure that the mission was sustainable, that we would have the foundation in our own house to do the important, vital work we do—from saving the Obama cats in Atlantic City to protecting species around the globe.

Of course, to always be ready to send out our teams when disaster strikes, we do a lot of advance preparation and planning. We have to be prepared for all sorts of contingencies. One of the most important things we do is to recruit and retain the best-trained people on our teams. We have built an amazing network of volunteers who are ready and able to respond on moment's notice.

We have also built a strong political network at the federal, state, and local levels, allowing us to respond quickly to their needs using appropriate protocols. We only respond to natural disasters—fires, floods, hurricanes, and so forth—when we're appropriately and officially invited in by local officials, so our local, regional, and state network is critical. We go into war room mode whenever there's a pending natural disaster, and we make sure in advance of those disasters that we're executing our mission.

As a humanitarian group, our partners allow our first responders to do God's work. If it weren't for our partners—including the wonderful Lois Pope, who has donated many trucks; Ellen DeGeneres, who donated a truck in partnership with the Walmart Foundation; Zoetis; Banfield Pet Hospital; the William H. Donner Foundation; the Kirkpatrick Foundation; and many others, we couldn't do what we do. These wonderful partners are humane heroes and angels for our cause. With their generous support, we have the resources required to create our national deployment model for animal rescue.

Just one example is our unique partnership with Zoetis. Zoetis is the largest animal provider in the world of animal health products and care, and we've built a longstanding relationship with the company. Whenever we deploy our rescue teams, Zoetis provides our veterinarians with all the medicines we need for disaster response, free of charge. This ranges from vaccinations and antibiotics to all sorts of medical supplies that allow us to work in our mobile clinics.

We're also there for animals in good times, not just bad. We are boots on the ground for numerous veterinary and shelter clinics. We provide underfunded shelters with the needed relief to ensure that the animals they house receive the veterinary care and triage efforts they need. We have used our trucks to deliver food to underprivileged communities, and we have conducted a number of pet clinics for homeless veterans.

Our trucks and the team members who work in them drive much-needed resources and veterinary care to communities all over our country, every day of the year. It's just one of the many things we do at American Humane, but I believe we do it better than anyone else. We are truly First to Serve.

## CREATING A MORE HUMANE WORLD

When I think about the future, I think that what we are seeing in communities across our country and even communities throughout China and Europe is a movement toward what I call a "humane lifestyle." There is a consciousness, an awareness of how we treat living creatures like there's never been before in the history of humanity. There is a tremendous amount of interest within the public for the humane treatment of animals, and I'm convinced it's all because we've had a mad, passionate love affair with our dogs and cats—especially over the past 20–30 years. As a result of this interest, we've seen a dramatic change for the positive for animal protection. You can see it in new laws and regulations that are being passed, you can see it in the consciousness of people globally, and you can see it in the ways that zoos, aquatic parks, and other such facilities have changed their practices.

At American Humane, I envision that, in the not too distant future, as people go about their daily lives and make humane choices, those choices will have been certified by American Humane. People will know what they are serving on their dinner table was humanely raised. They'll know animal stars in the television show or film or live show they're watching have been humanely treated. They'll know the animals in the zoos and aquariums they take their kids to have been treated humanely.

I see every interaction with every animal in our lives as a humane choice, and that humane choice is determined through the American Humane platform of programs. People will know animals are humanely treated because they'll see our name associated with each one of these choices.

As the interactions between people and animals grow more complex, our programs will evolve to meet animals wherever they are. Today, for example, folks are traveling more than ever before with their pets on commercial flights. In recent years, it has become apparent that this mode of transportation is fraught with risk for companion animals. We all remember the tragic stories of animals that were mistreated—or died—while being transported on airline flights. We have decided to work *with* the industry and its partners to make the lives of animals safer and better.

In 2018, for example, we teamed up with United Airlines, which transports more animals each year than any other US-based airline, to implement significant changes and improvements in their PetSafe transport program. Animal welfare experts, researchers, and veterinarians at American Humane thoroughly examined United Airlines systems, practices, and policies surrounding the transport of pets, and we provided them with specific recommendations to improve the transport experience for the hundreds of thousands of animals who fly with them each year.

People don't want to know what humane is in terms of the actual science, but they want assurances that American Humane is working with the world's top scientists, ethicists, and behaviorists to provide humane protections for all animals. It's our job at American Humane to ensure every animal is able to live a humane life, free of pain and suffering. It's also our job to educate those who aren't touched by animals about the value of all sentient beings. That's a critical part of our mission. Once people know animals, they love them, and they will protect them. That is, at the end of the day, what American Humane was founded to do 143 years ago. Today, we are continuing to do it all ways, shapes, and forms—for people, animals, and the world we share.

## HUMANE CHOICES, HUMANE VOICES

Our vision for the future is bold, audacious, and visionary. We are building on the historic strengths of this legendary institution, the lessons learned from our challenging past, and importantly, the real-life conditions of animals as they exist in our world today. We recognize the moral courage it takes to fight for animals in far-reaching places around the world, for the animals being mistreated and abused in our own hometowns in America. We recognize that every day, we humans make choices. We make choices as to how we vote, how we spend our time, and how we spend our resources. We make choices as to how we treat and value animals and the world we share. It's our vision at American Humane to be the change agent for society as a whole, leading and encouraging people to make every choice a humane choice.

Our original social contract with the animal kingdom was based on the Five Freedoms:

- Freedom from hunger and thirst
- Freedom from discomfort
- Freedom from pain, injury, and disease
- Freedom to express normal and natural behavior (e.g., accommodating for a chicken's instinct to roost)
- Freedom from fear and distress

I think the social contract needs to be brought up to date. Yes, the Five Freedoms still serve as the foundation of the contract, but there's more to it today. Again, you can't protect what you don't love, and you can't love what you don't know. Implicit in the new social contract is that humanity agrees to treat animals with the respect they so deserve. It's pretty simple: All animals deserve humane treatment. It's the right thing to do.

The social contract works in two directions: from people to animals but also from animals to people. We certainly know that animals enrich our lives tremendously. We at American Humane are constantly looking for new ways to unleash the power of the human–animal bond to benefit us all. With a lot of research and good old-fashioned hard work, we will create a healthy ecosystem, we'll find new cures for cancer, we'll implement new solutions to problems that affect people and all the creatures with which we share the Earth.

Our social contract is something that benefits animals *and* people. We're all in this together, so long as we all continue to share the face of God's green Earth.

## A HUMANE PATH FORWARD

Consumers are removed from agricultural production and animal husbandry, yet the overwhelming majority of consumers care about how their food is produced. That's an enormous opportunity for farmers and ranchers to tell their story about animal care. Unfortunately, we've seen producers be confronted by those who have coopted the word "humane," and who may have an entirely different agenda than animal welfare or do not believe farm animals can be raised humanely under any circumstances.

Why don't we take "humane" back? At American Humane, the country's first national humane organization, we run the longest standing farm animal welfare certification program, the American Humane Certified program. We aren't like other organizations that claim to speak for animals. We believe in animal welfare, and we believe that science—not emotion or misinformation—is the center of good animal welfare policy. That's reflected in our scientific advisory committee featuring nearly 20 veterinarians and animal-science experts.

Our vision is that farmers can provide affordable, humanely certified food for all Americans—which will allow producers to reclaim the word "humane" from those who attack agriculture or who want "humane" to be something only for the wealthy elite. Our scientific standards cover space, light, air, food, and water, and are based on the internationally accepted Five Freedoms. When these standards are met, consumers can feel comfortable and confident that animals are living a demonstrably humane life, and that farmers are indeed doing the right thing.

*continued*

Science-based policy is at the center of our program. We also believe collaboration, not contentiousness, is the basis of a good program. Farmers are and have always been the first-line stewards of animal welfare, and American Humane has a long history—going back to 1877—of working together positively with farmers and ranchers to ensure best practices. America has a safe, affordable food supply, and now consumers are asking to be assured that it is humane as well.

It's important that mainstream certification has a broad tent. There are other certification programs, whether independent or internal to a corporation, but these don't cover many animals, and the costs associated with these programs often make the products too expensive to afford for the average family.

In contrast, the goal of the American Humane Certified program is to provide what Americans want—a third-party guarantee that animals are treated humanely—while not driving up the cost for Americans who want to consume these products. Humanely raised food is not an elitist commodity. It should be accessible to all Americans. It should be the standard by which all animals are raised.

Currently, our program covers more than 1 billion animals in the United States, far more than any other certification program. We work with small, medium-sized, and major producers to ensure the welfare of nearly one in eight US farm animals, but there is a way to go in providing a humane guarantee to all Americans.

Science-based measures mean that both producers and consumers can trust in the solidity of the program. And consumers are very much looking for third-party humane certification. According to a recent poll we conducted of 6,000 consumers, 95% of respondents were concerned about the humane treatment of farm animals. 75% stated that they were very willing to pay more for humanely raised eggs, meat, and dairy products. And in ranking of the importance of food labels, "humanely raised" scored highest. Interestingly, however, more than half of respondents (55%) reported that products branded humanely raised were either not available (36%) or too expensive (19%).

There's clearly consumer demand for humanely raised products—and an opportunity for producers to fill it. Of the existing certification programs, you'll find some that cater to the wealthy or are financially backed by groups with food agendas. Ours is unique in that we want to be a broad, positive conduit between producers and consumers. Ours is unique as we want every animal treated humanely. Too often the word "humane" is used antagonistically to attack farmers and ranchers or look down at them—even though in our experience most farmers work hard and care for their animals. Scientific and evidence-based practices that are third-party verified are a way to show consumers that you're doing things right and that the naysayers are wrong.

The American Humane Certified Farm program is intended to celebrate and give thanks to American farmers and ranchers who not only put food on our families' tables, but who work to put the "heart" in heartland by providing food that is safe, abundant, affordable, and humanely raised under ethical, commonsense, and scientifically demonstrated standards.

Together, we can recapture the word humane.[33]

---

33  https://robinganzert.com/media-appearance/a-humane-path-forward/

# Author's Note

Friends,

When I started writing *Mission Metamorphosis,* no one could have predicted that in 2020, a global pandemic, brought to us in the form of the novel coronavirus, would wreak havoc on our very way of life and bring our economy to its knees. As I write this, the global economy is poised to shrink more rapidly than at any time since the Great Depression, leaving all organizations, nonprofit and profit alike, adrift in very uncertain times—times that are strangely reminiscent of when I first took the helm of American Humane in 2010, just after the Great Recession.

As you have seen throughout the telling of this book, the team at American Humane weathered the storm we faced 10 years ago by employing best practices, thinking ahead, and being prepared to make tough decisions. Today, we are ready to batten down the hatches once again and take on the headwinds coming our way. Just as before, we will adjust our expenditures as needed while staying focused on our priorities and our historic mission. We exist to be the first to serve animals wherever and whenever they are in need, and now more than ever, they need our help. To that end, at the outset of the crisis, we launched a "Feed the Hungry" fund to help animal shelters and rescues that were unable to raise the resources needed for basics like food, bedding, and litter.

Of course, we all know that animal welfare is of paramount importance. What too many ignored, however, were the failures of our social contract with animals that led to this rampant pandemic. COVID-19 is a direct result of the inhumane and unsafe treatment of animals. Wet markets, like those in Wuhan where the virus is thought to have originated, are devoid of animal welfare and biosecurity measures. As a result, zoonotic diseases can quickly jump from live animals kept in inhumane conditions to freshly butchered meat. By prioritizing animal welfare and protection in our post-coronavirus world, we can prevent similar catastrophes and build a more humane and ethical world.

If you are reading this book, take the lessons herein to heart; they are battle-tested for success. Know that we will come out on the other side of this unprecedented struggle stronger and more resilient. It is through compassion and kindness that we will build a better world, together.

Your friend,
Robin

# Acknowledgments

The story of *Mission Metamorphosis* and my time at American Humane these last 10 years is rooted in our historic mission and lifesaving programs. We exist to serve animals, wherever and whenever they are in need. It is what we have been doing since 1877. This book tells just one small chapter in our organization's long and storied history.

I am incredibly proud of our programmatic success—we improve the lives of some one billion animals around the world each and every year. That spectacular achievement is due to the hard work and dedication of our inspirational staff, volunteers, and donors.

So many people have contributed to improving the lives of billions of animals around the world through American Humane's programs. This book is a tribute to their fierce dedication, hard work, and advocacy. I am grateful to our governing board for their guidance and wisdom, helping to bring a landmark institution into the twenty-first century. Special thanks to Board Chairman John Payne, Vice Chairman Candy Spelling, Secretary Dawn Assenzio, and board members, including Bill Abbott, Dr. Brian Beale, Dr. Marty Becker, Amanda Bowman, Col. Scott Campbell, Debra Fair, Sharon Jablin, Naomi Judd, Rear Admiral Tom Kearney, Herbert Krauss, Dr. J. Michael McFarland, Lois Pope, and Abigail Trenk. John Payne and our board members share an enthusiasm for our mission and dedication to building a more humane world.

I would also like to thank my American Humane colleagues who devoted their lives to rebuilding this organization and delivering on the mission. Special thanks to Laura Sheehan, Mark Stubis, and Hayden Frye who helped make this book a reality. Their persistence brought this project across the finish line.

On a personal note, I dedicate this book and the stories to my precious children, Aidan, Jocelyn, and Robert, who I know will be the next generation of leaders in social impact. I am so proud of my kids and their love of animals. I am also eternally grateful to my parents, Rob and Linda Roy, who taught me the values of compassion, kindness, hope, and love. I am appreciative of my family, who are my source of inspiration, including my adorable fur babies.

I hope you will be inspired by these stories to build a more humane world.

With love and gratitude,
Robin

# Op-Eds and Select Media by Robin R. Ganzert, PhD

## SAVING THE ENDANGERED SPECIES ACT:
### *Protecting Some of Our Most Cherished and Most Iconic American Treasures*

The Endangered Species Act is itself now endangered.

There are currently several legislative and executive branch proposals to roll back the protections in the ESA, which for more than 45 years has safeguarded vulnerable species by restricting development that would disrupt their habitats, breeding, and existence.

Given that scientists now say we are facing a sixth mass extinction, with up to half of all species heading toward oblivion by the year 2050, animals need robust protections now more than ever. That's what makes these current plans to weaken this cornerstone of conservation policy so alarming.

Even in today's politicized environment, the protection of our animal species should be an ideal that unites Americans across the political spectrum. A national poll conducted by the Center for Biology Diversity finds that two-thirds of respondents want the ESA strengthened or left alone. Those who care about protecting our diverse wildlife must make their voices heard to defend this landmark legislation.

Proposed revisions to the ESA from the Departments of the Interior and Commerce would make it easier for development projects that threaten wildlife to gain approval as economic factors would be considered for the first time since the act was passed.

While we must always value, nurture, and protect our own human species, we can't—and shouldn't—put a monetary value on the survival of the remarkable creatures with whom we share the Earth. What price would we set, for instance, on the noble humpback whale, the mischievous southern sea otter, or the bald eagle—a living symbol of our country—which the ESA and American Humane helped save from the brink of extinction? For what do we profit if we gain the whole world and yet lose our nation's wild legacy and soul?

That doesn't mean that certain pieces of the law cannot be carefully updated or even improved through rational review and reasonable reassessments that take into consideration new science and evolving impacts on both animals and people.

While we do this, we should remember that the ESA's key elements have been successful at protecting some of our most cherished and most iconic American treasures, keeping 99 percent of listed species from going extinct. Scientists estimate that absent this vital act, at least 227 species would have likely disappeared. A 2012 study from the Center for Biological Diversity documented 110 species that have seen rapid recovery because of the ESA.

We supported the ESA's original passage in 1973 and support it again now, along with efforts to protect and preserve species in responsible zoological institutions that are serving as arks of hope for many of the world's remarkable and endangered creatures.

More than 1,600 threatened and endangered species now depend on the ESA for protection. Many will simply go extinct if we do not preserve the key elements of this vital legislation.

Humans, who are responsible for putting animals in this precarious state, must now band together to save them by saving the crucial protections in the Endangered Species Act.[34]

---

34  https://robinganzert.com/media-appearance/the-hill-saving-the-endangered-species-act-from
   -extinction/

# STOPPING INHUMANE VA CANINE EXPERIMENTS:
## Repay Dogs for Their Military Service

Dogs have a long history of military service, dating back to ancient times. Here in the US, canines have been used as scouts and trackers and to guard prisoners and deliver messages on the front lines since the Civil War. More recently in Iraq and Afghanistan, these four-legged heroes have employed their remarkable sense of smell to sniff out improvised explosive devices and weapons caches. In fact, these incredible dogs have given us their best. They have put their own lives on the line to protect and defend us.

So it is at once shocking and inconceivable that the front lines may be safer for dogs than the medical center laboratories of the Veterans Administration. Indeed, the Department of Veterans Affairs—still striving to recover from massive scandals involving its (mis)treatment of human patients—is now becoming embroiled in another controversy, this one involving its (mis)treatment of canines.

News reports published last week in this paper and elsewhere found that the VA is continuing to conduct invasive experiments on dogs as part of its medical research program, experiments that result in the euthanasia of the animals. According to the reports, there are currently nine active experiments at four VA facilities, including in Milwaukee, where researchers are removing parts of the dogs' brains to test neurons that control breathing prior to killing them by lethal injection, and in Cleveland, where doctors are measuring dogs' cough reflexes by placing electrodes on their spinal cords. When done, the cords are severed, killing the dogs.

## VA maintains that studies on dogs are necessary

Sadly, the VA is not alone in using dogs in the name of scientific research. Just as other institutions have defended this practice as critical to medical breakthroughs, officials at the VA maintain that their canine experiments are ethically sound and can lead to discoveries that can positively impact veterans suffering from paralysis, heart ailments, and breathing problems. They cite prior studies on dogs that resulted in the invention of an implantable cardiac pacemaker and procedures that led to the first successful liver transplant.

But that argument holds less water than what fits into a Yorkie's bowl, because according to the VA's own website, those discoveries date back more than a half-century, to the 1960s.

In an act of compassion, the US House of Representatives passed legislation last year to defund the VA's canine experimentation program, but the measure stalled in the Senate. Nevertheless, earlier this year a federal bill was passed that requires the Secretary of Veteran Affairs to first grant approval before any funding can be allocated to this research. And just prior to his dismissal, Dr. David Shulkin, the then VA secretary, issued a moratorium on any new experiments moving forward without permission and that all ongoing studies had to go through a formal review process by VA research leadership.

But these barriers haven't precluded or impeded the VA from conducting what may be painful and is definitely fatal research on dogs.

Please know that we are not advocating that all research be prohibited, because as one of us (Lois Pope) has learned from producing a new documentary, *Made for Each Other*, with award-winning filmmaker Ric Burns, there are enormously important groundbreaking studies being conducted at Duke University, using fMRI technology to determine dogs' cognitive abilities, with the goal of improving the ways they are bred and trained to help humans as service and therapy dogs. Also, because dogs can get the same diseases as humans, scientists at Cornell University are using canine DNA to improve the effectiveness of new immunotherapy treatments for cancer. These are but two examples of dogs being used safely in research that could be beneficial to humans.

American Humane, the country's oldest national humane organization, is supportive of positive prevention studies designed to keep animals and people healthy, and advocating in any work it funds that no animals are harmed, there is no induction of illness or injury, and they are not euthanized.

## Dogs serve us in so many other ways

It doesn't take a scientist to know that dogs can and do play an essential role in bettering the lives of all of us, and particularly our military and our veterans. Through our decades of activism and support of animals and disabled veterans alike, we have seen first-hand how dogs provide much needed assistance and therapy for veterans suffering from post-traumatic stress disorder. They also act as guide and service dogs for veterans who have been blinded or disabled in combat.

Working side-by-side with the men and women of our armed forces while putting their own lives on the line for our country, military dogs take loyalty to a whole new level through such service. By doing so, they have saved countless thousands of lives.

Now it's time that we do something to save their lives and those of all our four-footed friends by immediately stopping and banning all harmful VA research involving dogs. We know we're not barking up the wrong tree in saying that since dogs are our best friends, we can't be treating them like our enemies.[35]

## TO FIGHT CANCER, TALK TO THE ANIMALS

Cancer victims have new weapons in their battle against the deadly disease, but they don't come in the form of pills. Instead, as members of Congress learned Wednesday, they increasingly come in the form of four legs and a wagging tail . . . or even trunk.

Scientists traveled to Capitol Hill on Wednesday to reveal breakthroughs and discoveries about the healing benefits animals can have for cancer patients. The event was the latest in a special series of briefings by the Congressional Humane Bond Caucus on important advances and policy developments on how, with our help, people and animals can improve each other's lives.

---

35  https://www.usatoday.com/story/opinion/2018/11/10/veterans-administration-dog-medical
-experiments-animal-rights-column/1920877002/

Consider the pioneering three-stage Canines and Childhood Cancer (CCC) Study, launched by American Humane Association to rigorously measure the well-being effects of animal-assisted therapy on children with cancer, their parents or guardians, and the therapy dogs who visit them. Prior to this first-of-its-kind effort, there was no hard data linking therapy dogs to positive effects on cancer, though the anecdotal evidence was sizable.

The CCC study is ongoing, with clinical trials taking place at five hospitals across the country. So far, we've seen a host of positive physiological and psychological benefits for both patients and their families.

But dogs aren't alone on the front line in the war on cancer. The development of new drugs and the study of other animal genes are also offering new insights into disease prevention and treatment. For instance, scientists working with elephants at Ringling Bros. and Barnum & Bailey's Center for Elephant Conservation recently found a promising new avenue in the effort to win the battle on cancer.

Elephants have many times more cells in their bodies than humans, yet elephants have a much lower rate of cancer. This happens because elephants have about 20 times more copies of a particular cancer-killing gene. Now, scientists are in the process of taking what they learned from this discovery in elephants and using nanotechnology to create cancer-fighting and preventative drugs.

During his State of the Union speech last month, President Obama pledged a "new national effort" to find a cure for cancer. Obama compared the commitment to fighting cancer to President Kennedy's promise to put Americans on the moon more than fifty years ago. A "moon shot," as Obama put it, is exactly what we need to stamp out cancer once and for all. Coupled with the bipartisan effort in Congress to put more funding into cancer research, that goal just may be attainable.

Rep. Gus Bilirakis (R-Fla.) and Rep. Henry Cuellar (D-Texas), who launched the Congressional Humane Bond Caucus, have been working with their colleagues on both sides of the aisle to secure an increase in funding at the National Institutes of Health to help find cures and treatments for diseases, such as cancer. Both the private sector, through a coalition of biotech companies, doctors and researchers referred to as Cancer Moonshot 2020, and government officials are setting aggressive goals for the battle against cancer.

The toll cancer takes on families is heartbreaking. But hope is alive and well, and it comes from both our friends in the animal kingdom and those in the halls of Congress. For more than 1.5 million Americans diagnosed with cancer each year, and for the 40,000 US children now in treatment for the deadly disease, some of the best medicine might come, as Dr. Doolittle said, from talking to the animals—and learning from them.[36]

---

36  https://thehill.com/blogs/congress-blog/healthcare/270816-to-fight-cancer-talk-to-the-animals

# Index

# About the Author

R obin R. Ganzert, PhD, serves as president and CEO of American Humane, the country's first national humane organization and the first to serve animals in need of rescue, shelter, or protection. She is a highly sought-after public speaker and is regularly featured in the media as an authoritative voice on animal welfare, having appeared on *TODAY*, *World News Tonight*, CNN, and *Fox Business News*, among other programs. Her perspective has been featured in newspapers, including the *New York Times*, the *Wall Street Journal*, the *Washington Post*, *USA Today*, *Chicago Tribune*, *Los Angeles Times*, and the *Boston Globe*.